"In a culture determined to define beauty with a mirror, Heidi Goehmann turns our gaze to the Song of Songs to affirm that our wrapping is never as exquisite as the gift we have inside. This eight-week study is full of rich, biblical insights, needed humor, and powerful stories. This is hands down one of the best Bible studies I have had the privilege to walk through. Fresh, honest, and insightful, *Altogether Beautiful* will have women of all ages finding themselves in these pages. Regardless of how you viewed yourself before this study, by the time you turn the last page, you will see how God has uniquely knitted you *Altogether Beautiful*."

—**Donna Pyle**, speaker, founder of Artesian Ministries, author of *Forgiveness* (CPH, 2017) and *Without This Ring* (CPH, 2016)

"*Altogether Beautiful* is a rare combination of rigorous biblical study and relatable discussion questions; it takes a rather enigmatic book of the Bible and makes it clear and comprehensible. Goehmann paints a beautiful picture of Christ's love for us throughout this well-designed study. This will certainly bless and encourage individuals and Bible study groups."

—**Rev. A. Trevor Sutton**, author of *Authentic Christianity* (CPH, 2017), *Why Should I Trust the Bible* (CPH, 2016), and *Being Lutheran* (CPH, 2016)

"*Altogether Beautiful* invites connection on a personal level from the very beginning, and the life applications are deep, probing, and significantly relevant. Perhaps most important, the study conversation not only prompts self-examination but also inspires outward concern and consideration for others. Whether you are a forever-believer, a new Christian, a skeptic, or a seeker, you will find this book inviting and easy as Heidi comes alongside as a friend to make you want to dig into the Word; understand, apply, and learn it by heart; and discover new directions for prayer. You'll talk about beauty, vocations, relationships . . . and what happens when foxes get into vineyards!"

—**Pat Maier**, pastor's wife and cofounder of Visual Faith Ministry

"As the husband of Susan and father of three daughters, I consider the message of Song of Songs, as it is unwrapped and highlighted by Heidi Goehmann, to be as precious and necessary today as when Solomon penned it so long ago. The message is from God, and it is for each of us, but it is especially relevant to our wives and daughters these days: in Christ and in truth, you are altogether beautiful! This is the best study of the Song of Songs I have ever come across. Period. Well done, Heidi!"

—**Rev. Greg Finke**, author of *Joining Jesus on His Mission* (Tenth Power Publishing, 2014) and executive director of Dwelling 1:14

"Heidi has long written in such a way that she takes Scripture and sends it directly to the reader's heart. *Altogether Beautiful* is no exception. Not only does she delve into the many layers of this beautiful but sometimes intimidating book of God's Word, but she also points us to the most beautiful truth of God's love for His people."

—**Sarah Baughman**, author of the Regency Silhouettes series

"In today's society, it is easy to lose sight of God's love for us, but thankfully this study digs deep into the Song of Songs to show us women how deeply loved we really are. I enjoy how dynamic this Bible study is because it keeps me engaged and wanting to learn more. I have no doubt in my mind that you will feel the same!"

—**Madalyn Short**, Director of Family Life Ministry, Living Word Lutheran Church, Galena, Ohio

"Gazing at his ravishing bride, Solomon deems her 'altogether beautiful.' That acclaim befits this elegant Bible study by Deaconess Goehmann, who delves into true beauty—not as seen by the world, but as God sees us through His Son, Jesus Christ. The heavenly Bridegroom claims His Church as His Bride. He washes us in Holy Baptism, dresses us in His own righteousness, and invites us to dine at His eternal wedding feast. Instead of trying to make ourselves more attractive, we simply believe the Word of Christ: "You *are* altogether beautiful, My love" (Song of Songs 4:7, emphasis added)."

—**Rev. Dr. Christopher W. Mitchell**, author of *The Song of Songs* in the Concordia Commentary series (CPH, 2003)

"Heidi Goehmann artfully, and with wonderful personal touches, explores how the study of the Song of Songs can speak to women in our culture today. Exploring the relationship between a young woman and her lover, Goehmann reveals the many lies that prevent women today from being able to see the beauty of their own selves as daughters of the King. I highly recommend that you consider *Altogether Beautiful* for your next study. I have already recommended it to my wife."

—**Dr. David L. Rueter**, author of *Teaching the Faith at Home* (CPH, 2016); DCE Program Director at Concordia University Irvine; Youth & Family Ministry Facilitator for the Pacific Southwest District LCMS

"This study is an amazing, creative application of the Song of Songs to the personal life of the Christian woman. The author poignantly shows the chasm that sin brings in this beautiful relationship, causing endless struggles in the Christian woman about her attractiveness and desirability. The study is a refreshing call to reclaim the delight that God has in her so that she can embody this wonderful vulnerability and intimacy in her life."

—**Dr. David Ludwig**, licensed therapist, professor, and author of *Christian Concepts for Care* (CPH, 2014)

"*Altogether Beautiful* invites women to reconsider how we define beauty, love, vocation, and identity, in contrast to what God reveals in the Song of Songs. Heidi's honest, witty, and wise reflections draw the learner into a deep conversation of how the world sees her, how she sees herself, and how God sees her. *Altogether Beautiful* has flexible daily or weekly formats, with thought-provoking questions and online videos for group or individual study. Additionally, the notes on the Hebrew and Greek vocabulary add rigor, yet are accessible for everyone. I have been waiting for a study like this from CPH!"

—**Kimberly S. Loontjer**, Assistant Professor of Political Science, Concordia University Wisconsin

"Women of all ages and stages of life will enjoy the insight for relationships to our Savior, ourselves, our families, and our churches in this study. Whether you just watch the videos or do the five days of homework plus extras like the memory work, the author gives permission to make this study fit your life. The prayer prompts focus our prayers to deeper conversations with our heavenly Father on the topic we've just studied. The homework is a great mix of being in the Word to find what it says and asking ourselves to reflect on our own experiences and lives."

—**Kristine Wendorf**, wife, mother, and friend

"I grew up in a home where I was told I was beautiful. And I still struggled to believe it. Wasn't that just something parents were *supposed* to say? I often thought. As a parent now myself, I realize more and more that it's not just something parents say. It's something that is hardwired in us to see in our children. And that's what God sees in us. Reading through these pages of Heidi's gentle, encouraging, and true thoughts on this was so refreshing. To know that I am completely seen and known, and still loved and thought beautiful? Yes, please."

—**Leah Heffner**, blogger/podcaster at *Life Around the Coffee Cup*

"Heidi Goehmann wants us to see ourselves the way that God sees us. She quiets the lies that we tell ourselves and that the devil whispers in our ears by clearly showing the depth and breadth of God's love for us. Heidi's study is approachable and engaging, and reading it feels like she's in the room with us having a conversation about who we really are: His beloved."

—**Pastor Matt and Liz Schuler**, Holy Cross Lutheran Church, Oxford, Michigan

# Altogether Beautiful

A STUDY OF THE SONG OF SONGS
*by* **HEIDI GOEHMANN**

To Dave,
who points me to Christ
every single day.

Published by Concordia Publishing House
3558 S. Jefferson Avenue, St. Louis, MO 63118-3968
1-800-325-3040 ● cph.org

Manufactured in the United States of America

Library of Congress Cataloging-in-Publication Data
Names: Goehmann, Heidi, author.
Title: Altogether beautiful : a study of the song of songs / Heidi Goehmann.
Description: St. Louis, MO : Concordia Publishing House, [2018] | Includes
    bibliographical references.
Identifiers: LCCN 2017048959 | ISBN 9780758659934
Subjects: LCSH: Bible. Song of Solomon—Textbooks. | Christian
    women—Religious life—Textbooks.
Classification: LCC BS1485.55 .G64 2018 | DDC 223/.90071--dc23 LC record available at
hgps://lccn.loc.gov/2017048959

2   3   4   5   6   7   8   9   10   11            27   26   25   24   23   22   21   20   19   18

# Table of Contents

# Introduction

About two years ago, my husband put his foot down. It was a conversation we had had about a hundred times.

"How does this look on me?" I twirled around so he could get the full view of my aggressive clothing choice of bright blue shorts and a gray top.

He looked up from his book. "You look beautiful."

"Whatever—you always say that," I huffed, and I turned around to pick through my jewelry.

My husband is patient and peace loving. He's quick to listen and slow to speak. In our house, when he does say something, we tend to listen. So, what he said next is still etched in my memory, word for word.

"That's it. I'm not telling you you're beautiful anymore if you aren't going to believe me."

With that, he picked up his book and walked out of our bedroom. I was left standing, wondering. *Did I believe him?*

My mom told me I was beautiful every day when I was growing up. My dad would touch my hair at random and tell me how nice I looked, precious words I savored.

And there I was . . . married, thirty-five, and I still believed deep down that I was not worthy of the word:

## Beautiful.

Standing in front of the mirror, I looked at myself. My hips were wide, my hair unruly. I had no sense of style or color. I got angry too quickly, and words frequently came out of my mouth that would have been better off stuffed back in. I might be funny. I might be good at conversation. *In my heart, though, I believed I was anything but beautiful.*

My husband's outburst forced me to consider something I hadn't realized I had been avoiding for years. *Why, with all of the people closest to me telling me how beautiful I was, body and soul, did I stand in that bedroom in complete disbelief of their perspective? If I didn't believe them, whom was I believing?*

Somewhere deep inside, I had fallen for a lie fed to me by people I didn't even care about:

- the culture
- the media
- schoolmates I left behind long ago
- boys I didn't want to marry
- my own twisted ideas
- the lies of Satan, whom I knew to be the father of lies

The funny thing is this: after my husband put his foot down on the matter, I finally began to believe him. He was right. And it was time to start believing what God and those I was closest to said about me—that I was beautiful. My body housed the Holy Spirit. My form was created by Him. I was a steward of this vessel, and it was pleasing. And I certainly didn't want to pass on my intense struggle with my body to my daughters.

It was time to believe those whose opinions actually mattered to me. And I knew whose opinion mattered most. I knew who loved me most.

Like everything else in life, the answer to understanding and believing who we are lies in the Word of God. After that momentous day when my husband left me standing speechless in our room, I flipped through the pages of my Bible and prayed that God would release me from the unbelief that plagues womanhood for so many of us: that God could make me holy—worthy, even—in Christ, but never beautiful. In my study, I found the Song of Songs.

As I studied, I found that, of course, God gives us exactly what we need, in His time. He didn't give me a weight-loss program or a wardrobe makeover. *He gave me truth.*

## He calls me beautiful.

## "You are altogether beautiful, my love; there is no flaw in you." Song of Songs 4:7

I was created by God the Father, knit together carefully and with purpose. *You* were created by God the Father, knit together carefully and with purpose. I was redeemed by Christ. *You* were redeemed by Christ. By His sacrifice, God deemed me—and you—worthy vessels of the Holy Spirit.

As we open the Song of Songs, you'll discover that it has many messages. And while the book certainly isn't all about personal beauty, this is a message, I believe, He doesn't want us to miss. I pray you can hear the following truth as one of the many important truths we will discover in the Song of Songs, in God's Word. And that truth is this: you are beautiful, even when it's a challenge to believe it.

I wish I could meet each and every one of you in person. My two favorite things about Bible study are digging in to hear the truths of the Word from a God who loves and redeems me, and getting to share those truths in community. Our God created us to learn and grow with one another. Life just wouldn't be the same without others to share it with.

I'm genuinely happy you have decided to join me for study. I am blessed by each of you. I love to hear your thoughts, your insights, and your experiences. If you'd like to contact me, I can be found on my blog and website, ilovemyshepherd.com.

Many blessings, beautiful, beloved ones, as you study and grow!

*Heidi*

# How to Use This Study

This study is designed so that you can choose how much time and energy you feel you can commit at this particular season in your life. Maybe you're looking for a Bible study that will offer you the opportunity to go deeper and deeper into the Word. Maybe you'd like to start setting aside daily quality time with God, but you haven't been able to get there yet. Or maybe this season is a rushing wind blowing you every which way, and you just want to set aside a few moments to draw closer to the Savior. No worries! The study is meant to offer accountability while maintaining flexibility. Here are some options:

Option 1—Watch the video segments each week, either individually or with a study group. Videos can be found at cph.org/altogetherbeautiful. Use the Viewer Guide pages to take notes on the videos and for your personal prayers. If all you can commit to in this season is watching the videos and learning and growing, the Word is at work! Watching and discussing in community with others is also good for spiritual growth and understanding. If you don't have a group, consider inviting a friend to join you on the journey.

Option 2—Each week, there are five days of homework that expand on the videos. This may seem intimidating and time-consuming, but the homework is a great way to challenge yourself to be in the Word on a daily basis. Each day's homework should take about thirty minutes to complete. Some people like to sit down and do more than one day at a time; other people like to schedule a set time each day as study time; still others roll through a day's study work and skip questions that do not pique their interest, spending time on ones that do. You can commit to completing one day of homework or two, three, four, or all five days. This is grace based. Some weeks in life are busier than others, so I encourage you to complete what you can. God will speak through His Word, no matter how much homework you complete. You will not feel "behind" in the study if you miss a day.

Option 3—Dive in to all the "extras" included in the study: fun facts, Hebrew and Greek word study, the "extras" scattered throughout the weeks, and even coloring in beautiful artwork as you meditate on and memorize Scripture. Be creative with the text; share what you're learning on social media to add a message of hope to someone's day; frame the art found inside your workbook on your fridge or a wall in your home or office—put reminders all around you of God's Word and His redemption in Christ. The sky is the limit!

Do not get wrapped up in trying to find a "right way" to do this study. The goal is to take the Word of God into your heart each day, to take it off the shelf and hide it in your heart, to gain insight from the Word and from one another, and to come to Him in prayer and thanksgiving as you hear what He has to say to you: *you are free and beautiful in Christ Jesus!*

# The Empire of Solomon

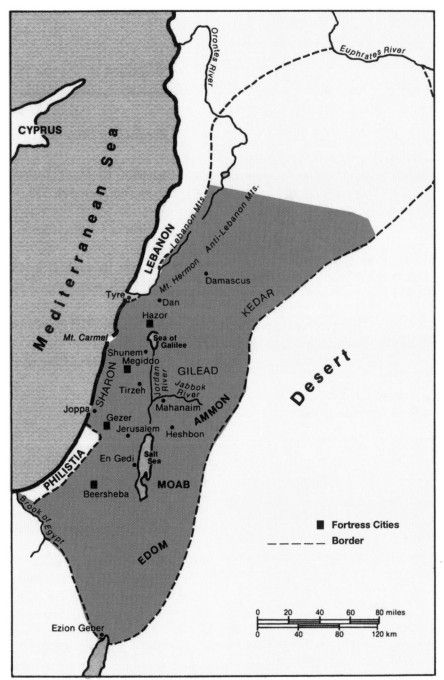

CYPRUS

Mediterranean Sea

Orontes River

Euphrates River

LEBANON

Lebanon Mts.

Anti-Lebanon Mts.

Mt. Hermon

Tyre

Dan

Damascus

KEDAR

Hazor

Sea of Galilee

Mt. Carmel

Shunem

Megiddo

GILEAD

Jordan River

Jabbok River

Desert

SHARON

Tirzeh

Mahanaim

AMMON

Joppa

Gezer

Jerusalem

Heshbon

En Gedi

Salt Sea

PHILISTIA

MOAB

Beersheba

EDOM

Brook of Egypt

Ezion Geber

■ Fortress Cities
- - - - Border

| 0 | 20 | 40 | 60 | 80 miles |

| 0 | 40 | 80 | 120 km |

# Useful Terms

**Allegory**—A metaphor in the form of a story or story image; the story on the surface has a hidden meaning underneath. This applies to our understanding of the Song of Songs in that the real story of Solomon and the Shulammite, their courtship, wedding, and intimate life contains the hidden but also real story of Christ and His Bride, the Church.

**Consummate**—The solidifying or completing of a contract or agreement. Consummation can be done with paperwork or a handshake. It is used legally and historically as the way the marriage contract is solidified. A marriage is commonly considered consummated when the couple engage in sexual intercourse. Completion and fulfillment are also associated with consummation.

**Hyperbole**—An exaggeration used to make a clear point; often accompanied by an exclamation mark.

**Incarnation**—The word we use to describe what happened when Jesus Christ came to earth as a baby boy, born of the virgin Mary in Bethlehem. Incarnation is when a deity, or god, becomes flesh. When we talk about Jesus' thirty-three years on earth, we call Him the incarnate Jesus. We celebrate the incarnation of Jesus on Christmas, when true God and true man came down to earth for our salvation.

**Intimacy**—The perception, state, or action of closeness. Intimate moments and intimate relationships are spaces in which you are vulnerable and reveal parts of yourself that you normally would not share in other relationships. Intimacy is generally reserved for family members, spouses, and close friends, but it can also occur with mentors, teachers, and even with strangers in moments of crisis or struggle.

**Metaphor**—A way of speaking in which the literal object or detail spoken about represents something else—for example, another object, relationship, or emotion. A metaphor not only represents something else but also is what it literally says it is. There are tons of possible metaphors in the Song of Songs, from vineyards representing intimacy and closeness to incense representing prayer. (I have big plans to ask God what represents what when I'm in heaven.)

**Old Adam**—A phrase we use biblically and theologically to define the sinful nature that is present in our personhood, also known as the old self. The old Adam is drowned and replaced with the new Adam in Baptism; but like so many theological concepts, the old Adam exists in duality with the new Adam until the day of Jesus' return, when we and all creation will be made new, completely and perfectly. So, we contend with the old Adam inside of us, warring with our new nature that desires wholeheartedly to follow Christ Jesus alone, rather than our flesh.

**New Adam**—Biblically, the new Adam is Christ (Romans 5:12–18). Christ does His work in us through the Holy Spirit, so we, then, are made new. We die with Christ in our Baptism and rise with Him through the washing of the water and Word as a new person, fully redeemed by Christ Jesus.

**Typology**—An understanding of biblical accounts in which a person or story prefigures or acts as a "type" of Christ. This is especially common in the Old Testament; for example, Jonah in the belly of the whale for three days serves as a type of Christ in the tomb for three days before His resurrection. Solomon and the Shulammite bride of the Song of Songs serve as "types," or prefigures, of Christ and His Bride, the Church (the whole Body of believers), in the New Testament, today, and in the new creation to come.

**Vocation**—A calling, professionally, personally, or in family life. People have many vocations: daughter, sister, wife, mother, teacher, neighbor, friend, pharmacist, barista, and so forth. These vocations are not our identity but rather areas of life in which we serve and are able to give glory to God. Vocations can change with seasons of life. Our identity never changes: we are children of God, redeemed by Christ Jesus.

**Vulnerability**—Our susceptibility to being hurt in a relationship. Making ourselves available to relationship can put us at risk: we could be hurt, there could be criticism, or the commitment to the relationship might not be reciprocated. In a relationship, we are vulnerable because while there are many benefits to starting a relationship or deepening an existing relationship, there is also the risk of pain and rejection.

# Week 1

## WE ARE INVITED TO DRAW NEAR

# Viewer Guide

VIDEO 1: DRAW NEAR
**SONG OF SONGS 1:1–7**

**VERSES TO BOOKMARK**
If you'd like, bookmark the following verses prior to starting the video so you can follow along in your Bible.

Song of Songs 1:1–7
Isaiah 43:4
Romans 5:8
Luke 12:6–7
Ephesians 5:28-29

The message of salvation and the promise of hope is the central message of Scripture. In every word, we find comfort.

In all of Scripture, there is a thread of grace that weaves throughout the

story of a _____ who _____ His people.

## SIX REALITIES OF THE SONG OF SONGS

1. It is _____.

2. It is _____.

3. It is _____.

4. It is _____.

5. It is _____.

6. It is _____.

**CANON**
The full set of texts chosen to be included in the Holy Scriptures; sixty-six books in total that make up the Old and New Testaments.

## SIX INTERPRETATIONS OF THE SONG OF SONGS

1. It's the love story of _____ and the _____

_____. (*Literal and Historical*)

2. It's a love story between an unknown _____ and an

unknown _____. (*Literal and Historical*)

3. It's a picture of _____ and His Bride, the _____.
(*Literal, and Typological or Allegorical*)

4. It's a picture of _____ and His love for _____.
(*Allegorical or Extended Metaphorical*)

**AUTHOR'S NOTE**
"Interpretation" here identifies themes woven into the story rather than ways we must view the Song. It also might be helpful to refer to the Useful Terms on pages 8–9 for definitions of *allegory*, *metaphor*, and *typology*.

5. It's the story of Solomon's great _____ in his kingdom and the _____ therein. (*Allegorical or Metaphorical, and Historical*)

6. It's the story of God's _____ for us as individuals. (*Allegorical and Metaphorical*)

**CHRISTOLOGICAL**
An understanding that all Scripture points to the saving work of Jesus Christ.

## SONG OF SONGS 1:1–7

## WHO IS THIS GOD WHO INVITES US TO DRAW NEAR?

HE IS A GOD OF _____.

Song of Songs 4:7: "You are altogether beautiful, my love; there is no flaw in you."

Isaiah 43:4                    Luke 12:6–7

Romans 5:8                    Ephesians 5:28–29

HE IS A GOD OF _____.

Song of Songs 7:11–12: "Come, my beloved, let us go out into the fields and lodge in the villages; let us go out early to the vineyards and see whether the vines have budded, whether the grape blossoms have opened and the pomegranates are in bloom. There I will give you my love."

*See also Hebrews 4:16 and Ephesians 2:4–9.*

HE IS A GOD OF DEEP AFFECTION, _____, AND DESIRE. (SONG OF SONGS 1:8–9)

*See also Exodus 20:1–6 and James 4:3–6.*

HE IS A GOD OF _____. (SONG OF SONGS 3:5)

*See also John 1:12 and Zephaniah 3:17.*

## DISCUSSION QUESTIONS

1. What are some of your favorite and very real people in Scripture?

2. Which of the six themes from the Song of Songs intrigue you the most? Which would you like to learn more about?

3. Go back and look, on your own or as a group, at the Scripture references under each characteristic of God listed in the last segment of our video study. Are any of the characteristics surprising to you or particularly encouraging?

# Day 1

I can never picture Solomon as one of those guys walking down the street, minding his own business. He seems larger than life to me. Maybe this is because I rarely hear his name without the title *King* attached to it. Maybe it's because he was birthed by King David and Bathsheba, two big names themselves. Or maybe it has to do with his position, power, wealth, and kingdom.

What do you know about Solomon? It's always fun to think back to the stories we read in Sunday School or discovered early on in our faith walk regarding these epic biblical characters.

Name one fact or story you recall about Solomon. (If this guy named Solomon is all new to you, that's wonderful! Feel free to write, "I have no idea who Solomon is!")

Whatever the reason, Solomon likely seems larger than life to many of us, not just me. Because of that, we often have a hard time picturing him as real. But he had real feet that walked, a real voice that broke in sadness and shouted in rage. He had real hands that reached out and held his wives (we'll hear more about that later) and children close. He had a real heart that cried out to God, that prayed and struggled. Solomon was real. To fully delve into the Song of Songs, we need to see him as a real person with real-life affections and emotions, wants and desires. God uses Solomon's realness, his place as a historical person who walked the earth, to give us, as readers of the Word, a closer look at life among His people during a very different time in history. In sharing the story of Solomon, God also gives us a sweet taste of His love and affection for us that crosses time and space.

It is important to note here that there are commentators who argue whether the Song is *about* Solomon or whether it is authored *by* Solomon. Those who argue this point are a small minority and not representative of most commentators. Why? We talked about this in the first video, but let's review.

Write out Song of Songs 1:1 below:

The text itself attributes the Book of Song of Songs to Solomon, so most commentators do as well. This is why many of your Bibles call the book "Song of Solomon." It's his song, written by him. It's also his story, lived by him, a man named Solomon. I use the title "Song of Songs," as many commentators do, because while the historical context of Solomon and his authorship is important, the Song really belongs first and foremost to God, as the most excellent of songs of His love.

Getting back to the life of Solomon, let's start by building the timeline of Solomon. This will help us place our feet firmly in the soil of history at the beginning of our study, instead of talking about the Song in vague ideas of "some people" "some time ago" "somewhere over there."

At one time, Solomon was a wee babe. Nothing like starting at the beginning. But we can go further back yet! Even Solomon's conception is recorded in Scripture for us. How life affirming! Please open your Bibles to 2 Samuel 12:24–25; it may be helpful to read the larger context by beginning at 2 Samuel 12:15 and reading through verse 25.

Who are Solomon's parents? What were the circumstances surrounding his conception?

Mother: _Bathsheba_        Father: _David_

Circumstances surrounding conception:

_Comforting his wife_

Now, read 1 Chronicles 22:6–16 to learn more details about the man Solomon. First, read 1 Chronicles 22:6–9 to find the meaning of Solomon's name. Fill in the missing words from 1 Chronicles 22:9 below.

"Behold, a son shall be born to you who shall be _a man of Peace & Rest_

_____   _____

I will give him _rest_____ from all his surrounding

enemies. For his name shall be Solomon, and I will give _Peace_____

_and_____   _quiet_____ to Israel in his days."

Rest, quiet, peace—there's a theme here. The name *Solomon* is related to the Hebrew word for "peace"—*shalom*. Shalom is not only peace, but a concept of wholeness wrapped up in calm, peace, rest, and well-being. God chose the name *Solomon*, indicating that the days of David's son's reign would look different from those during his own. When King David took the throne, he spent exponential time subduing the enemies of Israel. David fought valiantly for the throne, running from Saul, who forced him into skirmishes and battles, year after year. David's son Solomon would be given a gift: a reign of rest.

In our lives, too, God works His plans and purposes. Sometimes individual days feel like peace and rest, while other days feel like all-out warfare. Yet, every day, we are to live to His glory. Sometimes our days turn into seasons well lived on the battlefield, while other times we are offered a season of calm and rest. Often, our seasons of warfare and peace mix together, one battle here and some rest over there, rest now and then another battle tomorrow. Just as David's and Solomon's lives each testify to God's greatness, love, and forgiveness in very different ways, so do our lives.

Do you feel like your life has been more battlefield or rest? Explain.

How has God used your life to tell His story?

Continue reading 1 Chronicles 22:10–11. What charge does God give to Solomon through his father, King David?

*Build the house of the Lord*

Read on through 1 Chronicles 22:12–13 for a nugget we wouldn't want to miss. What three things does David urge or exhort his son to be or to do, through the grace of the Lord?

1. *Strong*

2. *Do not fear*

3. *" " Be dismayed*

David wanted more for his son beyond a desire to see the temple built. He also knew that for Solomon to complete the task of building a house for the Lord, he would need more than cedar, silver, and workers. David personally knew the challenges of establishing and leading a kingdom. He knew the pull of temptation, the desire to take the road that appears easier when the pressure is on. He knew the fear of failure. He knew doubt and loneliness. Because he knew intimately the joys and trials of kingship, David asked the Lord for gifts specifically for his son. He asked for discretion and understanding, something we may call discernment. He also asked that the Lord would help Solomon keep the law of God, because he knew the pain caused by sin. And he urged him to be strong and courageous, without fear—an echoing of his forefather Joshua when the Israelites entered the land of Israel, the land of promise, soon to be entrusted to Solomon.

**AUTHOR'S NOTE**
To see a fuller picture of David handing down his plans for the temple to Solomon, his son and successor, see 1 Chronicles 28:9–21 and 29:1–9.

David himself desired to build a house for the Lord, but the Lord told him that this task would fall not to him but to Solomon. As Solomon took the throne, as recorded in 1 Chronicles 28–29, David handed over his plans for this great temple, where the people of Israel would gather to worship, sacrifice, and sing praises in the presence of the Lord, the Most High God.

In 1 Chronicles 28:20, we see David's charge to Solomon once again.

"David also said to Solomon his son, 'Be strong and courageous, and do the work. Do not be afraid or discouraged, for the LORD God, my God, is with you. He will not fail you or forsake you until all the work for the service of the temple of the LORD is finished.'" (NIV)

David was up front about his concerns, and he asked God Himself and the people of Israel to support Solomon.

Read 1 Chronicles 29:1. What was David's apprehension about his son taking the throne and taking on the task of building the first temple for Israel?

*young + inexperienced*

Turn to 2 Chronicles 1:6–13 and read a classic account from the very first days of Solomon's reign. What did Solomon request of the Lord when offered the chance to ask for anything he wanted?

*Wisdom & Knowledge*

*Ability to Judge Well*

Wisdom and discernment are part of Solomon's testimony from the very beginning, and they will continue to be a thread as we follow him through his reign. Solomon will seek wisdom, give wisdom, and sometimes ignore wisdom.

Solomon and David stood as real members of a real family who carried out God's real kingdom work in their place in history. David messed up. Solomon, we will see, made his own mistakes. In 1 Kings 11, we read about Solomon's slide down the slippery slope of temptation, and it's heartbreaking. Our study today of who Solomon was would be incomplete if we shared all of Solomon's beautiful beginnings and none of his sorry sin—for Solomon's mess also made him that much more real.

Please read 1 Kings 11:1–12. What was God's command to the children of Israel, including Solomon (see v. 2)? Why does the verse suggest God put this boundary around His children?

*Do not*

Fill in the last sentence of verse 2 below.

"Solomon ___*Intermary*___

to these in ___*Love*___."

May we never cling to things in love that are not of the Lord.

# "Love the LORD your God with all your heart and with all your soul and with all your might." Deuteronomy 6:5

The good news is that God works in all of it: the good and the bad, our weaknesses and our failures. Despite Solomon's weaknesses and failures, the relationship of Solomon and this woman in the Song of Songs gives us the bigger picture of God's great love for us, of Christ's amazing love for His Bride, the Church. In our messes and in our strengths, in our discernment and in our struggles, God works out His plans and His story. That's one reason we have the Song of Songs to study together during these eight weeks. God saw fit to move a man named Solomon to love a woman, and with the pen of the Holy Spirit to write this love story, one like no other.

As we dive into the Song of Songs in the coming weeks, keep all of this in mind. Just as Solomon was real and walked this earth, we have a real, life-breathing God who wants to share Himself with us each and every day in His Word. *That* is altogether beautiful.

# Inscribed upon My Heart

Let's hide some of that Word into our hearts. At the end of each lesson, you will find the Scripture memory verse for the week. It may seem repetitive, but hopefully the repetitiveness will help make it stick. There will also be a prayer prompt unique to each day. Add the words of your prayer in pen, pencil, marker, or just in your thoughts.

I encourage you to use the Scripture memory verse for the week and the prayer prompt for each day to bring your confession, thanksgiving, praise, and requests before the God who calls you beautiful.

### WEEK 1 MEMORY VERSE

"Draw me after you; let us run. The king has brought me into his chambers." Song of Songs 1:4a

### PRAYER PROMPT

Father, You draw me after You in Your Word. Open my eyes to see . . .

> **ABOUT THIS VERSE**
> "Draw me" is no empty statement in the greater context of Scripture. Our great God invites us to draw near to Him, through Christ's death and resurrection, and He also invites us to draw near to Him daily in His Word.

### WHEN YOU PRAY . . .

If you're not sure what to pray, here is a potential outline for your prayers. Feel free to color outside the lines!

**Confession**—Presenting our guilt before God: broadly, that we are sinners, or narrowly, by admitting and presenting specific sins for Him to heal and forgive.

**Thanksgiving**—Offering our gratitude before God, through the Holy Spirit, for all that He has done for us and gives to us.

**Praise**—Recognizing God for who He is, such as Creator, Redeemer, Restorer, Defender, and so forth.

**Requests**—Sharing with God what needs you have, asking for help, seeking guidance, recognizing His hand in your life and in the lives of those around you.

# Day 2

## INVITED TO RELATIONSHIP
## SONG OF SONGS 1:1–4, 11

Song of Songs 1:1 can be translated from the Hebrew language with any manner of hyperbole.

"The Song of Songs, the loftiest and greatest kind."[1]

"The Song of songs, the Song (par excellence)."[2]

"The Best of Songs, which is Solomon's."[3]

"This is Solomon's song of songs, more wonderful than any other." (NLT)[4]

"This is the Song of songs, excellent above any others."[5]

Song of Songs 1:1 makes use of what we call the "Hebrew superlative."[6] It is a way that the ancient Hebrew language expressed hyperbole or high praise. The superlative is the highest form of something, the most, the greatest, the best. Think "King of kings and Lord of lords."

Look up the following verses to see a few examples of similar superlatives in action. Write the superlative you find next to the verse reference.

Deuteronomy 10:17

*God of Gods    Lord of Lords*

2 Chronicles 3:10

*Most Holy Place*

Psalm 136:2

*God of Gods*

The language of Song of Songs 1:1 in the original language is not holding back. It's simply the best song written: the Song of Songs.

Please turn in your Bible to 1 Kings 4:32. How many songs did Solomon write all together?

*1005*

*3000 Proverbs*

Wowzers! Solomon was a serious songwriter. It was clearly one of his God-given gifts. This makes sense, since Solomon was from a musical family. His father, David, played the harp, wrote numerous psalms, and frequently sang before the Lord (1 Samuel 16:23; 2 Samuel 22; Psalm 23; Psalm 108).

What gifts do you have? What gifts have been passed down to you by family members?

It's interesting to me that the Song has no introduction as to who the lovers in the text are. There is no back story, no cast list. Perhaps there was no need for this, as it is the greatest of songs, or maybe the people of the time knew more than we do now. Or perhaps the element of divine mystery has more place here than we would like. Whatever the reason, I think the fact that we know less than we'd like about the lovers helps us to apply the Song more broadly for ourselves. Sometimes we get so absorbed in a story, even a true one, that we cannot see God's message for ourselves in it. Illustrations are wonderful, but oftentimes we can choose to disassociate ourselves from the context so we don't have to exit our comfort zones and make any needed application to our own lives.

There's one more reason I believe the Song of Songs has fewer character introductions than we might like: neither the He nor the She is really the central person of the text. Instead, *the relationship* is the main character. Can you help a girl out and repeat after me for fun? *The relationship is the main character of this story.*

Read Song of Songs 1:1–4. What relational words or actions can you find, just in these four verses?

**AUTHOR'S NOTE**
When I talk about lovers in the Song of Songs, I'm not speaking of a sordid Hollywood affair or even "people who sleep together," as the term is often used in our current cultural context. I use the terminology *lovers* in the way it has been used in poetry for centuries—any romantic relationship, from a sweet and innocent courtship to a passionate and fiery marriage. We get to see the spectrum of this in Solomon and his bride in the Song.

This story of these two people—meeting together, pursuing each other, coming together, lamenting their mistakes and their flaws to each other—is less about the individuals and more about who they are in their oneness. If you are married, this reality might be a little easier to see, but even if you are not, think about the longing all of us have for something or someone to fill us. There is a reason phrases like "You complete me" and "Where would I be without you?" and "You make me whole" make many women weak in the knees—and why any of us cry and cheer as the characters in our favorite romantic drama *finally* figure out they were meant to be together. On some level, we identify the relationship as its own character, and we want it to fulfill its destiny.

Genesis 1 introduces us to our vertical relationship with God. Genesis 2 introduces us to the horizontal relationship of people, particularly men and women and families. Relationship is a beautiful thing. In the Song of Songs, we will get to see the beauty and mess of relationships in life together as it is laid out in the lovers' saga.

The idea that relationships are characters in themselves, with their own personalities and needs, particularly in marriage, is God's idea first. Read Genesis 2:20–25.

## "They shall become one flesh." Genesis 2:24

Turn to Song of Songs 1, settle back, and just read. Don't contemplate for now. Read the first chapter of this love story and hear the personality of the relationship. We'll wrestle with some of the intricacies of the phrases and the "events" in the coming weeks. For now, read and listen.

After reading Song of Songs 1, what words would you use to describe the relationship of the two lovers?

*Enchanted w/eachother*

In chapter 1 we also meet the "Others." These Others act as a chorus to support the Relationship. They have a vested interest in the "She" and the "He," but what they really care about is the "We." They want to see the relationship flourish and blossom.

What "Others" do you have in your life, cheering you on, especially those who know you well? If you're married, what Others do you have in you and your husband's lives, cheering you on in your marriage?

The Others only make an appearance twice in Song of Songs 1. You'll find the words of these Others below. Please fill in the missing words.

"We will ___ *delight* ___ and rejoice in you;

*e x4*

we will _____praise_____ your love more than wine

rightly do they love you." Song of Songs 1:4b

"We will _____Make you_____ ornaments of gold, studded with silver."

Song of Songs 1:11

"We will exult."

"We will extol."

"We will make."

These are words of support. The Others surround the Relationship with the encouragement it needs to grow. There are also times in our lives when we are called to be Others. We can be Others in the lives of individuals or in the marriage relationships around us.

Whom do you think you have been called to build up, love, and support in this season of your life?

_Family & friends   Church_

Choose at least two of the following references in Scripture and jot down what those verses have to say about how we can support the people and relationships around us.

John 13:34–35

_Love Each other_

Romans 15:14

_encouragement Teach_

Galatians 6:2

_Share_

1 Thessalonians 5:11

_encourage_

Circle the "one another" verse above that you might like to focus some attention on for this present season of your life. This may be one that you have been called to exercise frequently or one that you would like to practice more regularly. It may be one that God is using to poke at your heart, but you have no idea why just yet. Often He has ideas for our work in His kingdom long before we have the full picture in our heads.

C. S. Lewis also provides wisdom for us regarding relationships and loving one another in his book *The Four Loves*:

> To love at all is to be vulnerable. Love anything and your heart will be wrung and possibly broken. If you want to make sure of keeping it intact you must give it to no one, not even an animal. Wrap it carefully round with hobbies and little luxuries; avoid all entanglements. Lock it up safe in the casket or coffin of your selfishness. But in that casket, safe, dark, motionless, airless, it will change. It will not be broken; it will become unbreakable, impenetrable, irredeemable. To love is to be vulnerable. [7]

Who wants to live that way, giving your heart to no one and receiving nothing in return? While the heart might remain intact, it becomes trapped, all wrapped up in a tight little space. The Song of Songs lovers got it. The Others got it. Love is deeply embedded in us by a God who loved us first and most. He teaches us this in all He has done for us. He teaches us that loving others is always worth the effort, worth a celebration. It may hurt. It may leave scars. It may scream risk and work and effort, but without the vulnerability of investment, what would life look like? Dark and cold.

In the Song of Songs, one of the story lines we don't want to miss is that of a God who pours His love into the hearts of His people, creating a oneness—with Him and with each other—that we can only begin to contemplate. Praise be to Christ Jesus!

Relationship. It's an altogether beautiful thing.

## INSCRIBED UPON MY HEART

Use the Scripture memory verse for the week and the prayer prompt to bring your confession, thanksgiving, praise, and requests before the God who calls you beautiful.

### WEEK 1 MEMORY WORK
"Draw me after you; let us run. The king has brought me into his chambers." Song of Songs 1:4a

### PRAYER PROMPT
Father, thank You for the gift of relationship. Today, I pray specifically for . . .

# But Who Is She?

Do you find yourself wanting to know more about the two lovers in the Song of Songs? If you are at all like me, you are sitting there asking yourself . . .

## BUT WAIT! I KNOW A LITTLE ABOUT SOLOMON, AND ABOUT THE RELATIONSHIP, BUT WHO IS *SHE*???

Let's start with what we know. In Song of Songs 6:13, she is called "Shulammite":

> "Return, return,
> O Shulammite,
> return, return, that we may
> look upon you.
> Why should you look
> upon the Shulammite,
> as upon a dance
> before two armies?"

A Shulammite *may* have hailed from Shulem/Shunem, a village in the northern region of Israel, and was most likely from the tribe of Issachar. You can look at the map on page 7 to see this region's proximity to Jerusalem, where Solomon and the Shulammite would have resided as king and queen.

*Issachar*: The ninth son of Jacob, a tribe of the nation of Israel during the span of the Old Testament.

We know she was a woman being courted by the king, a bride of the king, and a wife of the king all within the space of the Song, so we can narrow "the Beloved" down to someone who at some point was the wife of King Solomon.

*She might be the Shulammite Abishag from King David's household.* Remember, Shulem/Shunem are believed to possibly have been the same village in northern Israel. If you are intrigued by this theory, look into 1 Kings 1 and 2. And while that might sound like juicy drama, no one is really sure if that's the case. *Or she might be the Egyptian pharaoh's daughter whom Solomon married.* To find out more about this woman's appearance in Scripture, see 1 Kings 3:1. Really, "She" could be any of Solomon's wives. Solomon, particularly later in his reign, had many other wives: seven hundred wives and three hundred concubines, according to 1 Kings 11:3.

The question we need to ask ourselves is this: Does it matter who this woman is?

## SOME THINGS GOD LEAVES UNREVEALED.

There are questions to which we will not have the answers, and that's okay. God knows the details, and so we sometimes need to leave the unknown in His hands. And while it's tempting to assume more than we know so we can pinpoint details and satisfy our curiosities, we draw near and rest in His lap. We sit down with His Word, with what we do know, and ask Him to help us set aside the things of lesser importance so that we can see His great message of love for each of us in Jesus Christ.

*Father, You know all things. Lord, we present our minds and our hearts before You. We ask that You would satisfy our hungry souls with Your Word and Your living water. Thank You for Your steadfastness in all things. Thank You for those who have gone before us, for their stories in the Scriptures that testify to Your marvelous works, especially the enduring message of Your Son, Jesus Christ. It is in His name we pray. Amen.*

# Day 3

## INVITED TO EMBRACE IMPERFECT
## SONG OF SONGS 1:2–4; 8:13–14

Let's understand another interesting component that could throw off our understanding of the Song of Songs—structure! You can't read the Song of Songs in a linear fashion. The book is not a timeline. That would be nice, and certainly easier to understand, but it wouldn't be nearly as poetic then, and maybe not as pretty and mysterious. So much of the Bible is a narrative, moving from point A to point B, from one account to the next account over a period of time. For instance, Genesis 1—in the beginning, God created light on day 1, the expanse of the atmosphere on day 2, and oceans and land on day 3, and so forth. God created Eve in chapter 2; the flood doesn't occur until chapter 7, and Joseph gets thrown into the pit in Genesis 37. Next, in the Book of Exodus, we read of Joseph's death, the Hebrews' enslavement in Egypt, and eventually the Israelites crossing the Red Sea. You can see it's a timeline of sorts.

The Old Testament as a whole, however, isn't a nice, neat timeline. Deuteronomy and Exodus tend to overlap a lot; Leviticus is in there somewhere; and the kings get chronicled not just in Chronicles but also in the Samuels and Kings as well. The books of the prophets, such as Jeremiah and Hosea, have timelines within themselves, but even those overlap at times. And Daniel and Isaiah have a lot going on all over the place.

In the New Testament, we reach the culmination of *all* time: Jesus' incarnation! He came to us as a baby on this earth. This was the moment all creation had waited for. And while the Gospel eyewitness accounts are sometimes parallel, we often find they vary in detail, for they were all written from different perspectives and in different styles.

The story, of course, doesn't end with Jesus' incarnation. Jesus gave His life for us on the cross. Then follow His resurrection and His ascension into heaven! And then the Church is born. Paul and the apostles reach up and out, north, south, east, and west. John is given a vision of the day when restoration will be far beyond our wildest dreams—the Lamb seated on His throne, a new heaven, a new earth. And the restoration—when Jesus returns to make all things new—is most definitely *not* the end of time as we know it (#toomanyapocalypseshows). The restoration is just the beginning of eternity with our Savior!

So, when we lay it out a little bit, you can see the Bible is linear and it isn't. Maybe this is because it's the work of a God not bound by our time and understanding. Maybe it's because so much in life is just not that simple. Very little in life is step 1, step 2, and then step 3. Planning, parenting, grief of any kind, and so much more is up and down and here again and back again.

Song of Songs allows us, or maybe even forces us, to step outside of a linear time frame and embrace the moment.

Read the Song of Songs verses listed below and label them as A, B, or C. Each label relates to the relationship of the She and the He in the text.

Most of these headings are from the cycles offered in *The Lutheran Study Bible* (p. 1067) and the Song of Songs Concordia Commentary, but they agree with several commentaries.

## LABELS[8]

A) The Invitation
B) Pursuing/Courtship
C) The Wedding/Consummation (and other "married people stuff")

Song of Songs 1:3–4 _invitation_

Song of Songs 2:8 _Pursuing_

Song of Songs 3:9–11 _Wedding_

Song of Songs 5:2–3 _C wedding people Stuff_

Song of Songs 7:11–12 _B · C_

Song of Songs 8:4 _C_

That was not an easy task! Well done! I'm not sure I could do this question justice if someone handed me the exercise and a Bible. It just isn't very cut and dried. It's all garbled up. Even for the Hebrew expert, it can be difficult to discern the structure of the Song. Most commentators agree that it is a *chiasm*—a poetic structure that follows a pattern that folds in on itself. It's like a sandwich: bread, protein, cheese, veggies, bread. If you are my husband, it would be more like bread, protein, cheese, protein, veggies, protein, bread. (The more meat the better!)

Here is an example of a chiastic structure from John 1:14–17, a Scripture reading I hear at my church almost every Christmas. This is one of my favorite examples of chiasm because it's a *grace* sandwich!

Of the Son from the Father A
grace and truth B
grace upon grace C
grace and truth B
through Jesus Christ A

The Song of Songs follows what I like to call a sloppy chiastic structure. It's not neat. A straight-up chiasm would be ABBA or, like the preceding example, ABCBA. The Song's structure, however, is much less organized, even though it includes the three basic themes we identified earlier in our study: Invitation, Pursuing/Courtship, Wedding/Consummation. However, the Song starts with C—Wedding and Consummation—and ends with C.

Read Song of Songs 1:2–4 and 8:13–14. What is the common activity in both sections?

*invitation*

Can you see the sandwich bread of the Songs at the beginning and end? The wedding and consummation is the great escape of the married couple. They are off together, casting aside the cares of the world for a moment.

What is your favorite way to cast off some cares? How do you relax, especially if you only have an hour or an afternoon?

Do you ever include a companion in your activities of enjoyment or rest? Who is most likely to join you? Maybe it's a spouse, a friend, or a loved one. Name your people for me.

The Song also has sections of Invitation, what we might label as A. This includes the man and woman seeking each other, searching for each other—their premarital courtship. This would be our cheese and toppings in our chiasm sandwich. In a narrative, we would normally think of the invitation as the beginning, but these segments are found woven throughout.

We cannot forget the meat in our sandwich, or sections we might label B in the chiasm. This involves the pursuing and the marital courtship of the lovers. The lovers are faithful to each other. Their marriage relationship isn't a drama of the back-and-forth "I love you, I don't love you." Rather, it's a poetic structure that might appear more like flash-forwards and flashbacks, reflecting beauty and keeping focus on the relationship experience rather than the timeline of the relationship.

In this way, the Song challenges us to take a step back and enjoy each word, each moment. It's not neat. It's not linear. Even if you have your Hebrew scholar hat on, the Song is different from translating a narrative text, such as Genesis or 1 Kings. It's not super clear where the middle is, or if there is one, and not all the chapters even have a sandwich; but the Song in its entirety does begin and end with C, and in the middle we find a lot of A and B and even the occasional C.

Confused yet? It's poetry. I love how my study Bible refers to it as "difficult poetry."[9] Many commentators identify the Song's poetry as one of the major stumbling blocks for anyone hoping to find the book's message of truth and its Christological center. Do not be daunted, precious reader. Hold tight. I think even this chaotic chiastic structure is a sweet gift of our Lord.

Some things in life weren't meant to be linear. Jesus' words in Matthew 6:34 speak beautifully here:

"Therefore do not worry about tomorrow, for tomorrow will worry about itself. Each day has enough trouble of its own." (NIV)

Much of the time, Jesus invites us to focus on just *this* moment, the time we have *right here, right now*. No more than this is guaranteed to us. The lovers in the Song of Songs understand this concept well, which I think you'll see more clearly over the next several weeks of our study. They take time for embrace and affection and contemplating the beauty of life—at least they do most of the time. And they certainly don't do it perfectly, but they do it well. The nature of poetry, in a biblical book, invites us to do the same—to focus on the beauty of the words, to take a moment apart from straight-up cognition to declare what is hard or what is beautiful or what is worthy of contemplation. What a gift from God! His Word, even when it is confusing and difficult, is altogether beautiful.

What is a favorite poem or song lyric that speaks to you? What is your favorite Bible passage that gives you encouragement for each new day? Sit back; enjoy the moment. Make a hot (or cold!) beverage. And share your thoughts below.

**MOST IMPORTANT, TAKE A MOMENT TO PRAISE HIM, WHO IS CERTAINLY WORTHY OF OUR EVERY MOMENT.**

## Inscribed upon My Heart

How are you doing with the memory work? It may help to write the verse of the week on a note card, a sticky note, or somewhere else where you can see it and have a reminder of God's Word and His love each week.

Use the Scripture memory verse for the week and the prayer prompt to bring your confession, thanksgiving, praise, and requests before the God who calls you beautiful.

### WEEK 1 MEMORY VERSE

"Draw me after you; let us run. The king has brought me into his chambers." Song of Songs 1:4a

### PRAYER PROMPT

Dear Jesus, sometimes life is not neat; sometimes it doesn't make sense. Help me to fix my eyes on You. Guide me in . . .

# Day 4

## INVITED TO THE FAMILY
### SONG OF SONGS 1:5–7

Brothers . . . who needs them? Clearly not the Shulammite woman.

To better understand the relationship between the She and her brothers, let's look at what we know from the text.

Please read Song of Songs 1:5–7. Then fill in the missing phrases of verses 5–6 below.

"I am very dark, but lovely,

     O daughters of Jerusalem,

like the tents of Kedar,

     like the curtains of Solomon.

Do not gaze at me because I am dark,

     because _____ _____ _____ _____

     _____ _____.

My mother's sons _____ _____ with me;

     they made me _____ _____ _____

     _____,

but my own vineyard _____ _____ _____

     _____!""

The Shulammite woman isn't just sun-kissed; she tells us she is baked by the sun. The term "mother's sons" in verse 6 is a pretty way of saying brothers. Some brothers are supportive. Some are funny. Some might be distant. The Shulammite says her brothers are angry brothers. The brothers' actions, sending the maiden into the fields for hard labor, do not seem loving and protective.[10] I find myself asking, "Why didn't you keep the vineyards yourselves, brothers?" The fields and vineyards can be dangerous, vulnerable to attacks when neighboring groups charge in to vie for territory and resources. Sending her to tend the vineyards appears to be a reproach at best, or a cruelty at worst.

I have to be up front. I happen to have a fond affection for the idea of brothers. I grew up with one brother. He was all grown and moved out by the time I was born, so I'm pretty sure I missed the muck and grunt of having to live with a growing boy. My fondest memories of my brother are of us staying up late, eating an entire batch of cookie dough straight from the mixing bowl, and watching hour after hour of old Marilyn Monroe films, with no shame. You can see where my vantage point might be slanted toward the positive side of life with brothers. I certainly have no memory of him forcing me to do yard work!

If you have brothers, what memories do you have with your brothers? Or what memories do you have with someone who is brother-like—perhaps a cousin or close family friend?

Has anyone else ever served in a "brotherly" role for you? Share a little about them.

My positive vantage point of brothers is great, but the Shulammite in the Song does not share my same sentiment. Thanks to her brothers, she struggles with feelings of insignificance, unworthiness, and shame.

## "I am very dark, but lovely. . . . Do not gaze at me because I am dark." Song of Songs 1:5–6

The brothers' actions, of forcing the Shulammite to work in the vineyard in their anger, and the earthly reality of the woman's situation or station in life are part of the chorus in her head.

Many of us can relate to this woman, struggling occasionally or often with questions and feelings of lower than or lesser than, in beauty and worth. Even when our families mean well, when they offer advice or offer to confront the struggles of life together, doubts and fears of inadequacy rise up. And to be honest, our families are the ones who can love us fiercest and cut us the deepest.

What messages did you receive about yourself growing up, positive or negative? Explain.

The People's Bible Commentary enlightens us to the difference between our own cultural perceptions of tan-darkened skin and those of the people at the time of the Song:
"Her dark, swarthy complexion stands in sharp contrast to the fair-skinned girls of the palace. Today a dark tan is often a sign of wealth, leisure, and beauty. For the ancients it was just the opposite. The wealthy and the nobility stayed out of the sun, while the lower-class people were forced to work out in the open."[11]

What kind of chorus do you have in your head when it comes to your worth? If it is a negative one, I encourage you to write out a prayer, laying it before the cross of Christ.

It's so easy to look at Christ's beautiful mercy and grace and think, "Am I worthy? Am I enough to receive what our precious Savior gives?" But creating such uncertainty isn't His intention. His resounding answer to us in Christ Jesus is YES! God declares you good in His creation of you. God declared you beautiful and worthwhile the moment He sent His son to this earth to die for you, and He redeemed you through the blood of Christ.

Yes, the Shulammite had some brother issues. In the New Testament, Jesus said something quite shocking about brothers that may be helpful to hear in light of all the imperfections of our families.

Read Luke 8:19–21 below, and highlight or underline Jesus' answer to the people in verse 21.

"Then His mother and His brothers came to Him, but they could not reach Him because of the crowd. And He was told, 'Your mother and your brothers are standing outside, desiring to see You.' But He answered them, 'My mother and My brothers are those who hear the word of God and do it.'"

This account is repeated by both Matthew and Mark. The biggest difference in Luke's account is the section you underlined. Luke gives us the amplified version of Jesus' words, an explanation of sorts: "This is *who* My mother and brothers are."

This passage gives us a broader picture of God's plan for *His* family, for all believers in Christ Jesus, that we, too, hear the Word of God and do it, meaning:

1) **We hear** His Word, the truth about who He is and who we are.

2) **We live** in the salvation it offers, which looks like confession, forgiveness, grace, and life together.

Our culture often preaches and teaches the words "Family's family." So, when our family lets us down or even leaves us battered and bruised, Jesus offers, as He always does, something more, something healing. Jesus says this to us: *"Let Me be your family; I am what you need. I give to you brothers and sisters and a safe place where love and forgiveness reign. I call this the Church."* The Church is often imperfect, but it was created by a perfect Savior as a means to offer one another real support. It's to be a place where we can hear the Word of Life about Christ's glorious redemption over every single piece of our lives. Through the Church we hear the Word of God, and we can be honest with Him about our flaws and weaknesses, honest with Him about the good and beauty He has created in us and through us.

Describe a time when your church family stepped in when you needed them.

When we feel less than beautiful, when we look around and lack support, we have somewhere and Someone to turn to. Read Song of Songs 1:7. Who does the Shulammite turn to after her admission of her darkness and family struggle?

## "Tell me, you whom my soul loves." Song of Songs 1:7a

We have Jesus. We have the triune God in Father, Son, and Spirit who tends to our souls daily by coming to us in Word, reminding us of the promises and assurance found in Baptism, and physically coming to us in Holy Communion. We can always turn to the One who is true, in prayer, in Bible study, and in Confession and Absolution.

Jesus sent the Helper, the Holy Spirit, to live and breathe inside of us. Our God never lets us down. We can run to Him. Like the Shulammite with her Love, we want to be where He keeps His flock, always in His pastures. Where He is, there we flourish. He tells us over and over that we are significant to Him. In Him, we are vulnerable and say:

## "For why should I be like one who veils herself?"
Song of Songs 1:7b

In Christ, we do not need to hide anything. We are made perfect in the Savior who gave Himself for us on a cross and walks on the road with us in our struggles. He comforts us in our heartache. He cheers with us in every one of life's joys.

It may feel at times like we have a split personality. We are just like the Shulammite. One moment we say with all conviction, "Yes! God calls His creation beautiful and that means me!" Other times we'll sink low: "Whoa, friends, hide your faces. This is one hot mess." But we *stand* on the truth.

We are forgiven, set free, and very much loved.

Our theme verse for our eight weeks of study is Song of Songs 4:7. Write that verse in the space here.

*Altogether beautiful*. When God looks at us, when He looks on our families and our churches, He sees Christ. He sees each of us, made new. Altogether beautiful, girls. Altogether beautiful. Take it to heart. You'll hear it a lot more, because we so often forget it.

Until tomorrow, stand in His truth, which is altogether beautiful.

## INSCRIBED UPON MY HEART

How are you doing with the Scripture memory verse for the week? Utilize the verse for the week and the prayer prompt to bring your confession, thanksgiving, praise, and requests before the God who calls you beautiful.

### WEEK 1 MEMORY WORK

"Draw me after you; let us run. The king has brought me into his chambers." Song of Songs 1:4a

### PRAYER PROMPT

Father, we thank You for creating us. We know that You call every piece of Your creation good. Jesus, we thank You for redeeming us. We are bought at a price, treasured by You. Spirit, we thank You for living in us, for carrying out Your work in our cracked and broken vessels, for healing and molding and shaping each of us in Your love. God in Trinity, I can see you at work in this broken world and in me when I look at . . .

# Day 5

## INVITED TO DELIGHT
## SONG OF SONGS 1:8–17

Terms of endearment—I'm a fan.

At the top of my list would be the term *darling*. It sounds classy and dignified. *Dearest* is another favorite, with its shorter counterpart *dear*, which makes me think of a good old-fashioned love letter. While romantic texts and Facebook wall posts might be a fun way to share love with someone, it doesn't seem quite as legendary as having a stack of letters bound in ribbon—letters your children will sort through after you have gone home to heaven and remember the love their parents shared on earth. There is a certain *je ne sais quoi*, as the French say, something fantastically indescribable, to an endearment well used. It captures a specialness for both the user and the receiver.

What are some endearments you have either heard, used, or wish you used?

The Song of Songs is rich with endearments. Read Song of Songs 1:8–17. List below the endearments you find.

Today, I want to settle on three particular endearments or descriptive words that Solomon uses regarding his Beloved in chapter 1: "beautiful," "my love," and "my delight." As we search throughout Scripture for references of these same words, we'll see more clearly how God, as the author of the Song through Solomon's pen, ascribes them to us, through Christ's sacrifice.

### Beautiful

I know I'm not the only one who frets about whether I'm beautiful. Beauty can be related to our spirits, our hearts, and our physical selves. Sometimes, I think we as Christians skip too quickly over physical beauty, for fear of making it more important than internal beauty. We can certainly put far too much emphasis on beauty that is fleeting, but God does work in both for His glory. Have you wondered at the mountains, a sunrise, or someone's hair? He is a creative God who makes beautiful things. It isn't vain to honor that.

*Beautiful* is a descriptor found in Song of Songs 1:8, twice in verse 15, and once again in verse 16. In the Bible, it's usually used to describe individual women, and even on occasion a man, but almost always people. It's another affirmation of how often God is thinking about people, how much He values them.

God creates beautiful things. God notices beauty, appreciates beauty, and makes what was not beautiful, beautiful in His way. Ecclesiastes 3:11 gives us a broader view of beauty in God's economy:

"He has made everything beautiful in its time. Also, He has put eternity into man's heart, yet so that he cannot find out what God has done from the beginning to the end."

We all have different things we wish were beautiful, things we ask Him to make beautiful. Some of us feel emotionally strung out. For some of us, the ugly in our lives is within certain taxing relationships. God promises in Ecclesiastes 3:11 above that He makes all things beautiful in their time. Do loss, war, tragedy, and the ugly things of this world ever make you feel hopeless or like a giant weight is sitting on your chest? Sin, death, and the devil can wreak havoc in us, in our relationships, and in the world around us. But God has promised to make everything beautiful. Anything we might look at and call ugly in life, know that He has the opposite planned for it—beauty . . . in His time.

He doesn't make just *some* things beautiful in His time. Read Ecclesiastes 3:11 again and fill in what He makes beautiful.

"He has made _Everything_ beautiful in its time."

What are you praying that He will make beautiful in your life?

What have you seen Him make beautiful in the past, in your own life or in someone else's?

Don't forget to include the beauty of Him taking our hearts, hardened by sin, and making them vessels bursting with love in Christ! I can't think of anything more beautiful than that.

## MY LOVE

רֵעְיָה
*rayah*: companion, darling, love, beloved bride

Solomon's next endearment is more of a noun than an adjective, but it is nothing if not descriptive. He uses this phrase in Song of Songs 1:9 and 15. The Hebrew root word in use here, *rayah*, has endearment written all over it. Honestly, I think I might just go home and pour a little Hebrew love on my husband.

*Rayah* is directly translated "darling" or "love." It's a sweet word, truly endearing, held close to the heart. Solomon showers affection on his Beloved with this language. He soothes her concern over her dark skin and her lowliness, her feelings of unworthiness. I can picture him softly rubbing her arm, the way my husband does when I'm really disappointed or feeling exceptionally inadequate. I can also picture my mom rubbing my back when I was disappointed and hurt as a young girl. Perhaps one of the greatest benefits of intimate relationship is being known at our worst and being loved anyway, with gentle care and warm embraces.

*Beloved* is the same endearment the Father showers on His Son, Jesus Christ, in the New Testament. Look up the following passages and describe the occasions on which God calls His Son, Jesus, "beloved."

Matthew 3:17 *My beloved Son / baptism*

Matthew 12:15–18 *Baptism*

Mark 9:6–8 *Transfiguration*

Jesus is beloved of the Father, no doubt. This affirmation is bestowed on us as well, in our heavenly Father's love for us through the Son. We are able to claim the intimacy of this relationship through our adoption as sons and daughters, heirs of the promise, in our Baptism.

What does Romans 8:14–16 have to say about our adoption, the Spirit, and our freedom?

Christ's death makes us daughters of the heavenly Father. Jesus' work signs our adoption certificates. We are beloved daughters in Him. You, my dear, are beloved of the Father.

The tiny Book of Jude, near the end of the New Testament, is just twenty-five verses. To whom is this short letter of Jude addressed? (See vv. 1–2 in the margin.)

**JUDE 1–2**
"Jude, a servant of Jesus Christ and brother of James, To those who are called, beloved in God the Father and kept for Jesus Christ: May mercy, peace, and love be multiplied to you."

Jude speaks to the Christians of the Early Church, but he is also speaking to you. You are valued by the Father, through the Son. You are called, beloved, and kept.

### Delightful

Please look to your Bible again and write Song of Songs 1:16 in the space below.

**FUN FACT**
The word *delightful* itself is really . . . well, delightful, don't you think? Other Hebrew words for delight include the following:[12]

עֹנֶג: *anog*—delightful or delicate, dainty

חֵפֶץ: *chephets*—delight, good pleasure

רָצָה: *ratsah*—take pleasure, take delight, approve, favor, enjoy

נָעִים: *na'iym*—pleasant, sweet sounding, or lovely, delightful

It's helpful to know the intimacy with which the lovers know each other in this particular verse. Scholars clarify the chiastic structure within Song of Songs 1 with the flow you see below.[13]

| | |
|---|---|
| Song of Songs 1:1–4 | Consummation, the complete union of husband and wife. |
| Song of Songs 1:5–8 | Courtship, the seeking for each other, the insecurity of new love. |
| Song of Songs 1:9–11 | Wedding; we read about ornamentation and jewels, which reflects a festival happening. |
| Song of Songs 1:12–17 | Consummation, again . . . the bread of the love sandwich. |

**MARRIAGE FEAST OF THE LAMB**
Won't that be a wedding to behold, when Christ comes back for us and unites with His Bride, the Church, and we celebrate for eternity?! Woozers! See Revelation 19:6–9 for more on this.

Delight is expressed between the lovers at its fullest when they can experience every part of each other. We will delight in our Savior fully, most completely, at the consummation of all time, the marriage feast of the Lamb and the never-ending delights of singing praise to Him in paradise. In that day, we will see Him face-to-face! What delight!

In the meantime, though, God knows we also desire to know that we are delightful to others now, here, in this time and place. Most days I am a bolt of lightning, a force to be reckoned with. In my best moments, I'm exciting—maybe—but I'm far from "delicate," which we often attribute to the term *delight*. Even those of us who are softer around the edges and mostly pleasant to be around are honored to hear that we are delightful. At the heart of delight is someone finding pleasure in something or someone.

In whom do you find pleasure? In whom are you delighted by their mere presence?

Who do you think finds pleasure in your presence?

Remember: God finds you absolutely delightful. Because of Christ we can stand in His presence, and oh, does He delight in us!

Please read Psalm 149:1–4 below and highlight or underline words that express delight, pleasure, or gladness.

"Praise the Lord!
Sing to the Lord a new song,
    His praise in the assembly of the godly!
Let Israel be glad in his Maker;
    let the children of Zion rejoice in their King!
Let them praise His name with dancing,
    making melody to Him with tambourine and lyre!
For the Lord takes pleasure in His people;
    He adorns the humble with salvation."

רָצָה
*ratsah*: take pleasure, take delight, approve, favor, enjoy

The NIV translation of the Hebrew root word *ratsah* has "takes delight," where the ESV translation says "takes pleasure" in verse 4 above. Our praises rise to Him and He takes utter delight in them. This is our relationship with the one holy and true God. That fact that He delights in *me* is wild! And I am so grateful. He wants to share time with me and with you. He invites us to do so by coming to Him in His Word and in prayer. He wants to be in our presence and invites us into His, through the grace of Christ.

Our relationship with God is a reciprocal relationship. Look at Psalm 37:4–7. What are we exhorted to delight in?

We have the opportunity to delight in God, who is so worthy. So worthy.

To wrap up today's study, let's take a moment to delight. Answer the following prompts and use them to share your thoughts and heart with the Lord in prayer.

Three words I would use to describe my God and Savior:

Three things I would like to thank God for today:

Three requests I present before the one who delights in me, and I in Him:

The introduction to the Song of Songs in my personal study Bible says it best:

"Life is more than precepts. God created us beautiful and passionate. To celebrate these blessings is to celebrate our Creator and His passionate love for us."[14]

Delightful. Beautiful. Beloved. Amen.

## INSCRIBED UPON MY HEART

Use the Scripture memory verse for the week and the prayer prompt to bring your confession, thanksgiving, praise, and requests before the God who calls you beautiful.

### WEEK 1 MEMORY WORK

"Draw me after you; let us run. The king has brought me into his chambers." Song of Songs 1:4a

### PRAYER PROMPT

Lord, I take delight in You, and I praise You for . . .

# Week 2

## WHEN I AM WEAK, THEN HE IS STRONG

# Viewer Guide

## VIDEO 2: THE PURPOSE OF PLEASURE
## SONG OF SONGS 1:12–14

**VERSES TO BOOKMARK**
Song of Songs 1:12–14
1 Chronicles 28:3–5
Romans 1:22–25, 28–32

Why are Christians so uncomfortable with the idea of _____?

What has happened in our culture is that we have relegated the good gifts of God to entertainment, fun, and recreation, when God created them to be experienced as _____.

## A BIBLICAL PERSPECTIVE OF PLEASURE

## (WITHOUT TAKING THE FUN OUT OF IT)

### 1. PLEASURE IS RELATIONAL.

We are meant to have pleasure in our relationship with _____.

The Lord takes pleasure in His _____.

The Lord takes pleasure in His _____ for us.

We are meant to have pleasure in our relationships with

_____.

We also are meant to have pleasure in other _____.

2. PLEASURE ALSO HAS BOUNDARIES.

_____ and pleasure do not belong together; they are incongruent.

God's design for pleasure never, ever is _____ or _____ to another person.

God is not inappropriately _____.

Pleasure points us to His _____, not ourselves.

## DISCUSSION QUESTIONS

1. Are there any topics that you wish were addressed directly in the Bible—such as loneliness, depression, sexual intimacy—but that you have not yet found a passage for? Discuss.

2. What pleasures do people find in married life? in friendships? in the family of God?

3. What other pleasures have we been given by God in this life?

FUN FACT ABOUT SONG OF SONGS 1:12–14

What of the words *nard*, *myrrh*, and *henna*? These are natural fragrances made from plants found in the Middle East or other lands delivered through trade during Solomon's reign and the Old and New Testaments as a whole. These oils and fragrances would have been used in wedding ceremonies and bring to mind the aromatics of intimacy for the reader of the Song both then and now. Nard was used by Mary when she washed Jesus' feet with her hair in John 12:3. These items are special and speak an uncommon honor to those using them. Commentators see the symbolism of this passage in many ways, such as the use of scents in worship of the Lord, prayer rising to God like incense, the Spirit and the Word working together to bring the Savior close to us, much as the myrrh lies at the center of the Shulammite's breast. Isn't that just it—God is a full sensory experience. He is close at hand. He treasures the prayers we share with Him. The fragrance of His blood in, with, and under the wine of Holy Communion speaks of the greatest intimacy—the giving of His very self to us. He is so beautiful.

# Day 1

The hallway was packed with people. My arms were laden with four textbooks, a few folders, and my gym bag. As I headed down the steps filled to the brim with fifty other middle school students, my shoe caught on the second step. Within milliseconds, I completely lost my balance. Books and folders flew everywhere. My body was staunchly disobedient to my internal pleas of "Grab ahold of something, anything!" and I completed my descent down the stairs in the prone position.

I woke up to a dozen faces staring down at me in shock and my gym teacher's gruff voice: "Graceful, Weirich, graceful."

I figured at that moment, if the floor could just swallow me whole, I would take it. I couldn't get up. My body was sore, my head ached, my spine felt like someone had taken a baseball bat to it. Before my graceful descent down the stairs, I didn't even know you could feel your spine. Spine awareness—it's a thing.

Classmates walking by kept stopping briefly to stare at me, because that's what humans do when they witness a train wreck. All I could do was stare back. It was awful. I have never felt more vulnerable in my life. Did I mention this happened in just the second month of middle school?

Little did my thirteen-year-old self know that vulnerability would be waiting for me around every corner of this life.

Most of us wish we could tell our old middle school friend, vulnerability, to get lost. Who wants to show their weak hand in the poker game of life? For so many of us, middle school was all about bluffing our way through and hiding our imperfections, even if it meant hiding very real parts of who we were. The truth is, for many of us, we haven't really left our middle school selves behind. How often do I hide my real self to stay safe?

When we are tempted to avoid connection in order to stay safe in this life, Song of Songs shares this insight with us:

# WHILE WE WANT TO HIDE OUR WEAKNESSES, GOD SEES THEM DIFFERENTLY.

# WHAT I CALL WEAKNESS, HE OFTEN CALLS STRENGTH, BECAUSE OF WHAT HE CAN DO WITH IT.

This week, we'll discover what the Song has to say about weaknesses. Read Song of Songs 2:1–2 and get ready to dig in deep.

In verse 1 the female voice states, "I am . . . a lily of the valleys." We can easily visualize a gorgeous Easter lily trumpeting Christ's glorious resurrection, but lilies of the valley, more likely referenced here, are a different thing. This flower is found close to the ground and is easily trampled on.[15] It's delicate and weak, a common wildflower. The message of this particular verse is not in the specialness of the lily or the rose, but in their plainness and—you've got it—vulnerability.

Imagine a giant sandaled foot clomping through the woods, right over this delicate little flower. Now you've got about the right image the woman from the Song is trying to convey. A simple step could leave her flattened beyond recognition. A strong wind could knock the vulnerable flower away from its stem, its lifeline to food and growth. This is how we also imagine weakness in our own lives. In my story earlier, you could probably easily envision the vulnerability associated with lying at the bottom of a flight of stairs, multiple sets of eyes staring at you, thankful to be in one whole piece physically but simultaneously dying a thousand emotional and mental deaths of embarrassment and shame.

Metaphorically speaking, we can spend our whole lives trapped in middle school, waiting for someone to reach out a hand and help a girl out.

What do you see as a few of your weaknesses? These can be professional, personal, something you are working on spiritually, anything. For instance, I'm a terribly impatient person. That's a weakness. I'm also easily concerned with other people's opinions of me. Weakness.

Write a few of your weaknesses in the space below.

> **FUN FACT**
> If you have heard the title "Rose of Sharon" attributed to Jesus, it comes from this one reference in Song of Songs 2:1. It is not found anywhere else in the Bible.

List the people in your life with whom you can share these weaknesses—people who build you up, who love you and encourage you. If you do not have those people, know that the heavenly Father sees and hears you. He builds and encourages better than anyone.

God puts people in our lives to shine the light of His Son into the vulnerable places of our lives. The Lovers in the Song of Songs are intimate enough that she can say, "I'm a lily of the valley. I'm weak. I need some work." In sharing her vulnerability with her lover, she invites him to know her more fully. When we share our weaknesses in our relationships, we are more fully known too. In being real and placing all the cards of who we are on the table, intimacy deepens and each person in the relationship can share more of him- or herself—weaknesses, warts, and all. It's a beautiful thing, albeit not always an easy thing.

When have you seen a relationship grow through weakness and difficulty?

Because of Jesus Christ, we can meet with God and abide in Him, as the Lovers of the Song abide together. God the Father invites us to share our weaknesses intimately with Him. What do each of the following verses tell you about our relationship with God the Father, Christ Jesus, and His view of our weaknesses?

Romans 5:6

1 Corinthians 1:26–27

1 Corinthians 12:21–24

In 1 Corinthians 13:12, God assures us that He knows us intimately and fully, when we only can see snippets and snatches of who we truly are:

## "For now we see in a mirror dimly, but then face to face. Now I know in part; then I shall know fully, even as I have been fully known."

He knows every strength, every weakness, every hairline fracture found in our minds, our bodies, and our spirits. And in our ongoing relationship with Him—sharing in His Word, remembering what He gave us in the water and the Word, and sharing in His body and blood—we get to know Him more fully, to love Him more fully, to be intimate with the Creator of the universe, the Savior of our souls.

In our intimacy with God, as we share our weaknesses in prayer and study, He responds as the Lover responds in Song of Songs 2:2:

## "As a lily among brambles, so is my love among the young women."

God takes our weaknesses and makes them strengths. "Oh, just a lily? I say a lily among thorns, among brambles, a beautiful, unique surprise tucked into the dark undercarriage that is this world." Our heavenly Father sees every part of us as altogether beautiful, a tiny miracle. To Him, we are anything but common.

Song of Songs 2:1–2 points directly to Christ as well. Turn in your Bible to Psalm 45 and find the Holy Spirit-inspired description beneath the psalm title: *To the choirmaster: according to the Lilies. A Maskil of the Sons of Korah; a love song.*

This connection may feel random to us, but be assured it isn't to God. Perhaps this love song with some lilies attached will help us understand the broader interpretation of Christ in the Song of Songs. Scripture really does interpret Scripture.

Underline the descriptors of Jesus Christ in Psalm 45:2–4 below.

"You are the most handsome of the sons of men;
   grace is poured upon Your lips;
   therefore God has blessed You forever.
Gird Your sword on Your thigh, O mighty one,
   in Your splendor and majesty!
In Your majesty ride out victoriously
   for the cause of truth and meekness and righteousness;
   let Your right hand teach You awesome deeds!

In 2 Corinthians 12:10, we discover what happens when we let Christ fill our holes of weakness. Circle the promise you hear in the verse below.

"For the sake of Christ, then, I am content with weaknesses, insults, hardships, persecutions, and calamities. For when I am weak, then I am strong."

God doesn't just give us strength in our weakness. Because of Christ, those very weaknesses are now strengths, and He will use them!

Look back to the beginning of this lesson at one of the weaknesses you shared. How might God use this weakness as a strength to do His work?

For when I am weak, then I am strong, for Christ's sake. Isn't that altogether beautiful?

## INSCRIBED UPON MY HEART

Each week has a new Scripture memory verse. You can find it at the end of each lesson. It may feel repetitive, but that will hopefully make it stick. There are prayer prompts for each day as well. Add the words of your prayer in pen, pencil, marker, or just in your thoughts. Use the Scripture memory verse for the week and the prayer prompt to bring your confession, thanksgiving, praise, and requests before the God who calls you beautiful.

**ABOUT THIS VERSE**
God is with us in every season of our lives, whether a joyful Indian summer or a winter of grief and struggle. He promises that winter will pass in a very literal sense, but also in light of eternity with Christ.

### WEEK 2 MEMORY WORK

"My beloved speaks and says to me: 'Arise, my love, my beautiful one, and come away, for behold, the winter is past; the rain is over and gone.'" Song of Songs 2:10–11

### PRAYER PROMPT

Lord and Savior, Jesus Christ, thank You for speaking to me in Your Word, especially . . .

# Day 2

## WEAKNESSES OF THE CHURCH
## SONG OF SONGS 2:3–6

My husband is the pastor of a joyful congregation. As a family, we are very active in our church, and I love knowing that the Body of Christ is a safe place where I can share my burdens, find forgiveness and acceptance, and be surrounded by a village to help teach and train up my children in the faith. But if I'm honest, church is also one of the places I can feel the most judged, the most out of place, and the most disconnected.

Yesterday we addressed our weakness and vulnerability as individuals. Today, we'll address it as a group, within the Body of Christ.

First, turn the pages of your Bible to Song of Songs 2:3–6.

Do you have the children's song "His Banner over Me is Love" stuck in your head? I do, thanks to verse 4 from our reading:

> "He brought me to the banqueting house,
> and His banner over me was love."

The phrase "His banner over me" is actually a military metaphor. To understand it fully, read Numbers 2:1–2 and fill in the missing words in the passage below.

"The Lord spoke to Moses and Aaron, saying, 'The people of Israel shall

camp each by his own _____,

with the _____ of their _____

_____. They shall camp facing the tent of meeting on every side.'"

The Hebrew word *diglo*,[16] from the root word *degel*, used here for the words "standard" and "banner," is only ever used in the Book of Numbers and today's passage from Song of Songs 2:4. It's an interesting connection, since the Book of Numbers records the Israelites' wanderings through the desert wilderness for forty years, long before Solomon's reign as king of Israel. In Numbers 2, God is readying the Israelites to conquer the promised land of

דֶּגֶל
*degel*: banner, standard, flag

Canaan. The banner was a representation of "their father's house," the Israelite tribe to which they belonged. According to Jewish tradition, the banner would have contained a visual image for them. It served as an active reminder of their identity as a chosen child of Yahweh, the one true God. Someone was in charge of carrying the banner for the Israelites of that clan to see. It was a reminder of God's refuge and protection over them, that He was very much present with them in the days of warfare and in the days of triumph.

In Song of Songs 2:4, the metaphoric military banner over her is love. This banner is a proclamation of their relationship and his protection and care for her. Just as the Israelites looked to the banner as a reminder that they were under God's care, so the Shulammite can be reminded of Solomon's care and declaration for her.

Weakness and vulnerability aren't just individual struggles, for they exist within communities as well. Warfare, strife, and political dissension speak particularly to community vulnerabilities and weaknesses.

The Israelites as a corporate group of people were vulnerable. Imagine them wandering the desert for forty years. What trials might they have found? What people or things do you think the Israelites needed protection from when conquering the Promised Land? (For a clue or two, check out Numbers 11, 13, 14, or 20.)

What arguments do you think the Israelites had? Do you remember some from reading the Old Testament?

The Lovers' intimate sharing of weakness and vulnerability is not only true for individuals before God but for the Church on earth before God as well.

What relationship does God identify between Christ and the Church in Ephesians 5:22–23?

Because Jesus Christ is the Head of the Church, like a husband is to be the head of his wife, we call the Church, the Body of all believers, "the Bride of Christ." The Church was created by God but also was redeemed by God. In both creation and redemption, He makes it clear that it is treasured by Him. One day the Church will also be completely restored by God, along with all creation. Until then, she has to bear the effects of sin in this world, just as we do as individuals. While the invisible Church is perfect in Christ, the visible Church, that which we can see physically and understand, will reflect weaknesses until Christ comes back for us. That doesn't make the visible Church less worthy of our time or energy. In fact, remember, Christ values us and comes for us while we are still sinners (Romans 5:8); and so, we value the imperfect Church as our family of God. Yes, the Church is vulnerable on the inside as well as the outside. But it is used by Him mightily, often in its weaknesses, just as we are as individuals.

Name a weakness of the Church, something the Body of Christ struggles with, within your family of believers locally or as a whole throughout the earth.

What does the Church need protection from, especially things that come from outside the family of believers?

**INVISIBLE CHURCH**
The whole compilation of true believers in Christ Jesus through time and history.

**VISIBLE CHURCH**
The group of individuals that I define as church because they profess belief in Jesus as their Savior.

His banner of love, His protection, His strength in our weakness, is not only over us as individuals, but also over His family—the Church.

That disconnection I mentioned I sometimes feel at church? That is a weakness of every church, because every church is filled with people who will always be sinners, even though we are all saved by the grace of Jesus Christ. There will be times when I feel lonely because of people's actions, but also just because I'm looking to heaven, and this earth will never quite be enough. In the same vein, churches will always struggle with how to best use people's time, treasures, and talents, and this struggle may even lead to ugly conversation at times, words that require confession and reconciliation in the forgiveness of Christ, because anything that matters can lead to heated conversation and hard decisions. In all of the Church's weaknesses, God promises that He is at work.

Look through the following verses. For each one, identify God's protection promise to you as an individual and also to the group of members, that is the Body of Christ.

PROMISE FOR THE CHURCH          PROMISE FOR ME

2 Corinthians 4:7–10

1 Corinthians 12:24–27

Psalm 46:1–3

Now look back at Song of Songs 2. Read through verses 4–6 again. Where does the Lover bring the Beloved in verse 4?

God invites each of us, as members of the Church, His Bride, to the banqueting house, to come and meet with Him in prayer and worship. This invitation is extended because we are under His banner. Jesus Christ is our identity, and He has claimed us as His beloved. In the banqueting house, He offers us forgiveness in the bread and wine that we share together at His table (Matthew 26:26–28). How cool is that?! Just as the Shulammite asks her Beloved to sustain her with apples and raisins, we are sustained, we are refreshed, because He offers us His precious body and blood and His Word. Song of Songs 2:5 points us back to the bread and wine we receive in Holy Communion and also to the Word, which is our daily bread.

What is our response to this goodness offered? We can't get enough. We want more of Him and less of us. He is the lover of our souls, the filler of our hearts.

What is the last line in Song of Songs 2:5?

*Sick with love* . . . My study Bible calls this "love-induced weakness."[17] Yes! The value of weakness is that it brings us to our knees before God. As a Church and as an individual, when we spot our weaknesses, we are at the best place to come before God in humility and ask for His help.

Martin Luther explains Song of Songs 2:5–8 in this way: "'Hence,' he says, 'I ask this because my whole being is on fire with the love of my God out of this consideration of His blessings.'"[18] *On fire. Alive in the secure love of Christ.* Martin Luther was certainly a fiery character at times. He knew the heat of fighting for things that mattered, of fighting the good fight to share God's love and His Word with others. But most of all, he knew God's grace in His own life and saw that grace work in the lives of those around him. God's grace sets a fire burning inside of each of us that cannot be quenched. Knowing that we are fully and freely forgiven, all shame is gone, the tomb is empty, and life is ours. And so we cry out with the psalmist:

"For great is His steadfast love toward us, and the faithfulness of the LORD endures forever. Praise the LORD!" Psalm 117:2

He is so faithful.

We are so loved.

We are sustained. The weaknesses that we see in the Church today are made beautiful in His tender affection. Altogether beautiful.

## Inscribed upon My Heart

Use the Scripture memory verse for the week and the prayer prompt to bring your confession, thanksgiving, praise, and requests before the God who calls you beautiful.

### WEEK 2 MEMORY WORK

"My beloved speaks and says to me: 'Arise, my love, my beautiful one, and come away, for behold, the winter is past; the rain is over and gone.'" Song of Songs 2:10–11

### PRAYER PROMPT

Father, You call Your Church "Bride" and "Beloved." Please guide my local church . . .

# Day 3

## WEAK BOUNDARIES, DESTRUCTION BRINGETH
## SONG OF SONGS 2:5–10

Have you ever heard the phrase "Let sleeping dogs lie"? I attest that this proverb really should read, "Let sleeping babies lie." When my oldest son was born, he could sleep through just about any noise: the vacuum, the blender, you name it. But the one thing that would wake him every single time was the doorbell. We even made a sign and posted it next to the doorbell: "Please knock, unless you'd like to rock the baby back to sleep yourself." No, we didn't really put that on the sign. Rather, it gently suggested that the guest knock because the baby was sleeping. But I sure did feel like adding some snark sometimes.

Sleeping things certainly should be left to lie.

It's time for the Song of Songs to impart some direct wisdom about waking and sleeping to us. This wisdom is of a far more serious nature than my lighthearted doorbell story because it has to do with love, the human heart, and purity. Reach into your arsenal of human experience and think about the wisdom you would share with someone on these topics.

What bit of advice would you share with a young girl in love or looking for love?

The writer of the Song of Songs addresses his wisdom poetically to the largest audience in the book, the Others. Read Song of Songs 2:5–10 to get a full picture of the scene.

> "I adjure you, O daughters of Jerusalem, by the gazelles or the does of the field, that you not stir up or awaken love until it pleases." Song of Songs 2:7

Please read verse 7 two more times. You could even read it aloud, to focus your mind on this important verse.

Yesterday, we talked about the fire that love is. It makes us weak in the knees and desperate for more. The message in Song of Songs is that this fire is a good thing, a blessing in our relationship with God and in the relationship between a husband and wife. However, I think we can all agree that in our current cultural context—in our world in general—we could really use some free advice:

# DO NOT AWAKEN LOVE BEFORE ITS TIME.

Love is not a game. Emotional intimacy and physical intimacy offer so much good, so much pleasure, so many gifts. But this intimacy is also meant to have boundaries, and if we awaken the sleeping beast before its time, we are in for a mess of heartache. Our bodies will reap the physical consequences, but our hearts are likely to feel the consequences for far longer.

Look at Song of Songs 2:7 again. What are the first three words declared by the writer?

The ESV translation uses judicious wording, whereas the NIV uses a slightly stronger phrase: "I charge you." Can you hear the adamancy of these words? We will see that this refrain is repeated in the Song of Songs three more times. "I charge you" is a message the writer wants the reader to take notice of. The Hebrew is related to the swearing of an oath. It's more than a flippant phrase that can be easily broken on a whim or by the shifting sands of ideas. Oaths in the Bible were very serious and binding. By using the phrase "I charge you," the speaker in the Song of Songs invites the daughters of Jerusalem into *accountability*.

Roland Ehlke, the author of the People's Bible Commentary on Ecclesiastes and the Song of Songs, notes that the pronoun "you" in "I charge you" or "I adjure you" in verse 7 is a masculine pronoun in Hebrew, even though it is most likely the female Beloved speaking.[20] This points us to a possible metaphorical or typological meaning in the charge for the reader: Christ has a time planned for when He will come back for His Bride, the Church, and that time is meant to come on its own. Just as we must be patient for firing up passionate earthly love in the proper time, so we must wait for the proper time for Christ's coming with patience. Two meanings in one phrase calls for some deeper study.

Let's first explore the literal meaning: the love between a man and a woman. Remember the context of these verses about love. We aren't talking about the nurturing love of a parent or the love for one's neighbor. We are talking

הִשְׁבַּעְתִּי
*hišbatî*: I charge, swear, take an oath, adjure[19]

about passionate love, a fiery love. We might characterize this love as set apart by one word: *desire*. This love was meant to be experienced in its fullest only within the context of marriage.

Why is it unwise to stir up passionate love before its time?

When we open a relationship to desire, we are undoubtedly and quite literally "playing with fire." I'm full of idioms today, but follow me on this for a moment. Pretend we have a box labeled "Desire and Passion." Once married, you open the box.

What wonderful things happen when desire is expressed in marriage?

Desire and passion expressed and fulfilled in marriage expands intimacy. The marriage relationship is a safe space. You can be your absolute self, naked and unashamed. You share your needs, reciprocally, as one flesh. You pursue one another and enjoy one another. It's imperfect, yes, but there is a level of safety and security in the design of marriage. It's a good gift of the Father.

Now that you have opened the box, the room called marriage is filled with the passion that was formerly inside that neat little box. Are passion and desire something you can stuff back into the box? No. They are ideas and expressions and experiences, not tablecloths and bedsheets that can be folded up and stored in a closet. You cannot neatly slide them back in, tape up your box, and move on with life. Passion works in marriage because it moves back and forth between two people in absolute emotional safety. Inside my own marriage, I'm not concerned with what my husband is going to do with my passion and desire. I know he will treasure it, hold it close, and share his own with me.

When we open a relationship to desire outside the bonds of marriage, *we stoke a fire we cannot contain.*

As humans, we mess up all the time. We say things that don't offer security to our spouses. In the worst of situations, when adultery happens, passion and desire are flung in all directions like flaming arrows that Satan uses to devour people and homes and hearts. Premarital sex has similar, even if less obvious, consequences. It leaves marks on our hearts and lives from trying to put that desire back in the box after it's been opened.

But in our complete and utter inability to hold strong to this wisdom, God has another plan: Jesus.

When sin enters in, when desire controls and heartache happens—as it most certainly will if love is awakened before its time—God gives us Jesus to show us His perfect, sacrificial love on the cross. And with Christ enters forgiveness, life, and healing.

In 1 Corinthians 13, God shares with us what Christ's real love and desire for us look like. It declares the *perfect love* of our Savior. These are good things to seek in our relationships, but more than that, the truths in this passage tell us about our Lord. He embodies perfect love without fear or flaw.

We are loved by this Savior's perfect love, and we are given the Spirit to go and share that, loving beyond how we think we can love, beyond our own purposes, our own gain.

Fill in the blanks below for 1 Corinthians 13:4–7.

Love is _____     Love is _____

Love does not _____     Love does not _____

Love is not _____     Love is not _____

Love does not _____     Love is not _____

Love is not _____     Love does not _____

Love does _____     Love _____

Love _____     Love _____

Love _____

Which aspects of love stick out to you the most? What is something new you discovered about Christ's love for you?

What was that first blank that you filled in? Write it again here.

Love is patient. It does not open the box of passion or desire before its time. Song of Songs 2:7 also strangely references gazelles and does, as in deer, female deer. What is that about? Christopher Mitchell points out in his commentary of the Song that these animals are anything but predatory: "Love,

First Corinthians 13 declares the *perfect love* of our Savior, a Savior who embodies perfect love without flaw.

"Love is patient and kind; love does not envy or boast; it is not arrogant or rude. It does not insist on its own way; it is not irritable or resentful; it does not rejoice at wrongdoing, but rejoices with the truth. Love bears all things, believes all things, hopes all things, endures all things."

like the Gospel, is gentle and rejectable. You cannot force love upon or out of another person."[21]

It's okay to say no, and other people have that right as well.

We need more of saying no in this world, for there are times when love should not be awakened. We need to set boundaries for touch in dating relationships. In married relationships, we need to recognize the slow fade of emotional affairs—choosing to eat lunch with a group of co-workers rather than that one guy; and husbands and wives need accountability when it comes to texting and emailing with their friends' spouses. We need to say no to things like pornography and sexually graphic movies. They mess with our emotions, our desires, our versions of what is realistic, and—quite literally—our brains. They do not honor the person on the screen, nor do they honor anyone sitting next to us. It's for those reasons that we put in place boundaries where they are necessary and good and safe.

God knows all about waiting. He knows all about patience. He knows all about yearning. Galatians 4:4–6 lays bare the patience of God, His wisdom in not awakening things before their time:

"But when the fullness of time had come, God sent forth His Son, born of woman, born under the law, to redeem those who were under the law, so that we might receive adoption as sons." Galatians 4:4–5

And because we are "sons," God has sent the Spirit of His Son into our hearts, by which we cry, "Abba! Father!" Sexual sin, the explicitness of what we find in the media, and our own lack of boundaries at times remind us that only God is pure, only God is holy.

"But when the fullness of time had come . . ."

"Do not awaken love until it pleases . . ."

God understands time and its boundaries. He also completely understands passion and desire. In His unquenchable desire to save us, He sent Christ, His precious Son, at just the right time. And His Son will come back for us at just the right time. We have forgiveness now. However, sometimes we need to know that God is familiar with waiting. It is no mistake that the Song of Songs addresses both the necessity of not waking love before its time and God's promises in the waiting.

Let's read further. Please read Song of Songs 2:8–10.

## "Behold, He comes."

Oh, He is coming! The images of the beloved leaping over the mountains,

> **REVELATION 1:7**
> "Behold, He is coming with the clouds, and every eye will see Him, even those who pierced Him, and all tribes of the earth will wail on account of Him. Even so. Amen."

bounding over hills, this is how great God's desire is for you, for each of His children, for His Church and His people. This is altogether beautiful.

## Inscribed upon My Heart

How are you doing with the Scripture memory verse for the week? Use the verse for the week and the prayer prompt to bring your confession, thanksgiving, praise, and requests before the God who calls you beautiful.

### WEEK 2 MEMORY VERSE

"My beloved speaks and says to me: 'Arise, my love, my beautiful one, and come away, for behold, the winter is past; the rain is over and gone.'" Song of Songs 2:10–11

### PRAYER PROMPT

Thank You, Lord, for loving me, for sending Christ at just the right time, for forgiving me, for coming back for me. I pray over love and boundaries . . .

# Day 4

## WEAK SEASONS
## SONG OF SONGS 2:10–14

Arrivals, the ways in which we first greet each other after a time of absence, are important. Dr. John Gottman, author and marriage researcher at the University of Washington, describes "harsh startup" as a discussion that begins with criticism, contempt, blame, or—you've got it—general harsh tones.[22] This may sound like a dramatic and rare instance in relationships, but the reality is that it happens in our homes all the time.

In life, certain seasons are more vulnerable to harshness than others. I remember when my first two children were very young and we had just moved. I felt extremely lonely. I was assaulted by emotions in what felt like the never-ending task of caring for my children's needs. As much as I loved them and knew how important this vocation of mom was, I had little joy in the day-to-day of mothering. It was a snapshot of time; it passed. But when I was in it, it was very hard. I remember time after time my husband would walk in the door and I would hand him a child and just cry. Things would immediately come out of my mouth:

"Take this baby."

"You're never here."

"I feel so lonely."

"I need more help."

"You don't care."

> **VOCATION**
> A calling, professionally, personally, or in family life; one of many roles we each have in this life, such as daughter, sister, wife, mother, teacher, neighbor, friend, pharmacist, barista, etc. These vocations are not our identity, but are areas of life in which we serve and are able to give glory to God. Vocations can change with seasons of life. Our identity as a child of God, redeemed by Christ Jesus, never changes.

I wasn't wrong in expressing my needs and my feelings, but I was wrong to accuse my husband unfairly. And to make matters worse, during that season of life, those were most often my greetings to him when he came home from work. My husband works hard. At the time, he was a new pastor, trying to build relationships. He did help out at home, and he tried his best to make time for us. In my desperation, though, I attributed all of my challenges and struggles to him, thinking it would make me feel better for a moment. It never did. As sin and hurtful words do, they only brought on guilt and shame. My husband never complained, but harsh startup can create an environment where a spouse dreads coming home or loved ones avoid connection because they don't want to endure the oncoming assault in the first five minutes of conversation.

What are other ways that people greet one another less than warmly?

Name your favorite way to greet someone when you see them, or a favorite way in which you have been greeted.

Open the Scriptures and read Song of Songs 2:10–14. How does the Lover greet his Beloved in verse 10?

קוּם

*qum*: rise, arise, stand, stand up, erect, establish

The word *arise* in verse 10 is from the Hebrew word *qum*, associated with a covenant. The word insinuates strength given through relationship.[23] The Lover is reaching out to His Beloved, offering relationship. In this we see again that Relationship is the main character throughout the entire Song.

How would you restate the Lover's words as a good but realistic greeting for someone you love today?

If Solomon is a type of Christ, a representation from the past of something to come, then we can apply the invitation of the Lover as an invitation from Christ to His people. Look for words of invitation in verses 10–14 and write them below.

Christ offers invitation to us throughout Scripture. One example is in Matthew 11:28–30. What does Christ invite us to share with Him in this passage?

This offer to come to Jesus is based in the firm knowledge of the covenant of His sacrifice for us on the cross. What does this new covenant give us according to Hebrews 9:14–15?

Fill in the title given to Christ Jesus in Hebrew 9:15:

"the _____ of the new covenant"

Christ's relationship with us was never meant to be one and done—Baptism and then little or no connection. He died on the cross, rose from the grave, ascended to heaven, and now *continues* to mediate for us. We never need to be concerned that He will revoke His promises when we lay down our burdens and our junk in His lap. He desires for us to bring our burdens to Him. He can handle our harsh startup, all our burdens laid out before Him, no matter how ugly they seem to us. No matter how long we have strayed from faith or neglected our relationship, He is there with open arms (Luke 15:11–32). He is always ready with His forgiveness, loving us through this life to the next.

What burden would you like to share with Christ right now? If you do not feel particularly burdened, share a greeting with Christ today.

Rest in the knowledge that He hears you. He has walked His own road of struggle and pain. He is at work in every piece of our lives. He also loves sharing time with us in relationship. And ideally, we relish time spent with Him, as the Lovers in the Song relish their time with each other. Christ's love for us is not dependent on our responses, but because relationships are so much fuller when the participants greet each other frequently, share time, and expend energy together, think how much richer our relationship with Christ is when we greet Him weekly in worship, meet Him daily in the Word, and spend time with Him in prayer. In Song of Songs 2:13, our God invites us to come away with Him. He tells us how much He loves to hear our voice and the voice of Christ, our mediator:

## "Arise, my love, my beautiful one, and come away."

There is one more voice that speaks on our behalf. Read Romans 8:26–27, and identify this voice that is at work in your life and relationship with God.

Every day we need the mediation of Christ and the Holy Spirit in our lives; but there will be times of pain, struggle, and sadness when we need to know beyond a doubt that this too—whatever "this" might be—shall pass. There is another promise we do not want to miss in Song of Songs 2:12–13.

Reread Song of Songs 2:12–13, and write down every promise you read.

**ABOUT MEDIATION**

"In the same way, the Spirit helps us in our weakness. We do not know what we ought to pray for, but the Spirit Himself intercedes for us through wordless groans." Romans 8:26 (NIV)

"Who is to condemn? Christ Jesus is the one who died—more than that, who was raised—who is at the right hand of God, who indeed is interceding for us." Romans 8:34 (ESV)

Have you ever had a winter in life? a difficult season? a darker time? God reaches down in these verses and assures us that everything has a time. Winter serves its purpose. The rains and snow are necessary to water the earth. But this season also has its "sell by" date. The Lovers in the Song proclaim the truth that Christ brings us from winter to spring:

"The winter is past; the rain is over and gone. The flowers appear on the earth, the time of singing has come." Song of Songs 2:11–12

Take a moment to acknowledge that the time for singing and for blossoming has indeed come in Christ. He gave Himself up for us. The work of our salvation is complete. Hallelujah! Yes, we will still have winters this side of heaven, before He comes back for us and brings full restoration. But those dark times in our lives have no real power, girls. Sadness and struggle will exist, yes, but Satan's destruction is not invited to this party. Spring is coming in Christ. Winter with the promise of spring is now-and-not-yet prophecy. Winters of life exist, but spring is fully ours in Christ. We are resurrection people. Amid the sadness and struggles of life, we rejoice that we live in the reality of Christ's resurrection. The Lovers in the Song rejoice in the vibrant sunlight, and we, too, rejoice in the light of our Savior, Jesus Christ.

Some winters are long and hard, and some are mild. It's okay to acknowledge that we need to hear that promise over and over again. We want to hear that spring will come. This is one reason we turn to His Word, even to odd little books of the Old Testament, in our daily journeys. It is there in God's Word that we hear the promise: there will be a time for blossoming (Song of Songs 2:13).

"The steadfast love of the Lord never ceases; His mercies never come to an end; they are new every morning; great is Your faithfulness." Lamentations 3:22–23

Lamentations 3:22–23 is also a covenant-filled passage. The Hebrew root translation[24] that we see as "never ceases" includes "does not vanish," "is never finished," "does not perish," and "will never be exhausted." The Lord will not desert us in our trouble. He will not desert us in our loneliness. He will bring the time for blossoming, growth, learning, and completeness. He comes for us across the hills and through the valleys. He calms the storms. Let us rejoice in Him! His promises to us are altogether beautiful.

## INSCRIBED UPON MY HEART

Use the Scripture memory verse for the week and the prayer prompt to bring your confession, thanksgiving, praise, and requests before the God who calls you beautiful.

### WEEK 2 MEMORY VERSE

"My beloved speaks and says to me: 'Arise, my love, my beautiful one, and come away, for behold, the winter is past; the rain is over and gone.'" Song of Songs 2:10–11

### PRAYER PROMPT

Gracious Savior, You promise that the winter will pass and the spring will come. Take my burdens, Lord . . .

# Day 5

## WEAK RELATIONSHIPS
## SONG OF SONGS 2:15–17

Life is busy for most of us. If you are reading this day's homework, that is most likely a sheer miracle, or a huge testament to your willpower. Much of the time, even when we are intentional and quite well-meaning, life gets in the way. Things get derailed. Schedules get moved around.

The experience of the Lovers in Song of Songs is no different. The "little foxes" of life easily get into their vineyard. The big question is, what does the damage look like?

Let's review all of Song of Songs 2 to get us started today. As you read this chapter, list all the items of creation that are used as descriptors or metaphors surrounding the Lovers and their experiences.

Now, focus on verses 15–17. Fill in the missing words from the ESV translation.

"Catch the foxes for us,
  the little foxes
that spoil the vineyards,

  for _____ _____ _____ _____

  _____.
My beloved is mine, and I am his;
  he grazes among the lilies.
Until the day breathes
  and the shadows flee,
turn, my beloved, be like a gazelle
  or a young stag on cleft mountains."

The vineyards, our lives, aren't desolate; the blossoms speak of lushness, growth, and health in our lives. They aren't filled with weeds, overgrown, and out of use. Praise the Lord! Let's take a minute to appreciate that. In our relationship with God, in Christ, there is life and abundance in every place. There are times when we will feel like a spiritual desert, times when the storms feel like they are rocking the peace we have in Christ, times when we will doubt and fear. But these are feelings, not truth.

One thing you will notice in the Song of Songs as we read through it is this: the Lovers are not outside of trial, they are not outside of the turbulence of emotions, and they are not outside of the responsibilities of their vocations and roles. Thankfully, the abundant vineyard that is Christ Jesus in our lives is steadfast. It just is. God tells us so in His Word, even when we can't see it.

Write John 15:1 below. Who is in charge of the vineyard of our faith?

God's Word is always purposeful. Scripture consistently uses vine and vineyard language where our relationship with and connection to Jesus Christ are concerned. Many of the metaphors used in the Song of Songs are only found within the song, but the vineyard and its abundance is one area where we need not doubt the message of God's love and affection in our lives.

What kind of "foxes"—false beliefs, myths about God, everyday pesky distractions—get into the vineyard of your faith, your connection with God?

The truth is that foxes get into vineyards. They eat the harvest. There are all kinds of "little foxes" that break into our relationships in life and try to tear up our vineyards. Beyond the message of your relationship with your Savior in the Song of Songs, there is the message about an actual relationship between the man and woman and the foxes. These foxes, from distractions and busyness to blow-out arguments, get into the vineyard of their marriage relationship, just as they get into everyone's relationships. The Lovers in the Song speak truth:

## "Catch the foxes." Song of Songs 2:15

Some foxes leave only ghostlike footprints of fear and doubt; some nibble at our fresh green leaves as annoyances; other things wreak havoc, tearing up vines, stealing the spoil, and leaving us to wonder if the vineyard is salvageable. Again, we turn to the Word to find out where God is in the midst of the vineyard, the foxes, and the aftermath of their destruction.

Because God is a grower, He not only keeps the vineyard of our relationship with Him stable in His Son, but He also gives us tools to grow the vineyard and protect it from the foxes. What tools? Let's look to the Word.

First, the primary tool! See John 14:25–27. Who is this Helper? What does He give?

What gifts does God offer us in 1 John 1:8–9? How might these be beneficial in our human relationships and in protecting those vineyards?

**2 CORINTHIANS 1:3–5**
"Blessed be the God and Father of our Lord Jesus Christ, the Father of mercies and God of all comfort, who comforts us in all our affliction, so that we may be able to comfort those who are in any affliction, with the comfort with which we ourselves are comforted by God. For as we share abundantly in Christ's sufferings, so through Christ we share abundantly in comfort too."

See 2 Corinthians 1:3–5, printed in the margin. What difference do God's compassion and comfort make in our relationships on earth?

Finally, read Ephesians 6:10–18. List the tools given as part of the armor of God. Beside each tool, write how it might be useful in guarding our relationships with God and with others from the foxes that want to spoil the vineyards.

Through the Word of Life—the Bible—and through direct communication with God in prayer, we are fed and filled up. God has blessed us with things like compassion, confession and forgiveness, and understanding and mercy—all through the work of the Spirit in our hearts and minds. Our relationships are intended to be a testimony of God's love not only to the individuals *within* the relationship but also to those *around* the relationship.

What relationships have you been *within*, or a part of, that have shared God's love and truth with you, have helped you to grow in faith, and have guided you in protecting the vineyard?

When have you simply been blessed to be *around* a relationship that was a testimony to God's love and work between two lives? Name the individuals of that relationship and share how you saw God real and active between them.

The Lovers in the Song of Songs know that some relationships are meant to be special, to be treasured and kept private. The Lovers know and testify to the specialness of the marriage relationship in particular. It isn't a small thing. The Bible refers to the male and female marriage partners as one flesh in Genesis 2. The Beloved proclaims this kind of belonging in Song of Songs 2:16:

## "My beloved is mine and I am his."

This kind of belonging exists because it is a reflection of Christ and His Bride, the Church—another reason Song of Songs shines with the typological interpretation of Christ and this Bride. When we talk about marriage, we can't get around the connection marriage has to Christ and His Bride, the Church, because earthly marriages are always meant to represent the greater picture.

Glance through Ephesians 5:25–32. What language of belonging do you hear in these verses?

Oh, He is so faithful! I need not fear my weaknesses and imperfections because Christ covers all of my relationships in His faithful forgiveness.

Song of Songs 2:17 also offers one more hidden promise to hold on to in this discussion. Read this verse again to have it fresh in your mind.

Christ will return for us, for His beloved. He will rise over the cleft of the mountain, on the clouds of the sky, for His Bride. My beloved is mine, and I am His . . . for all time and all eternity. Foxes have nothing on a Savior who died and rose to make you His own. That is altogether beautiful.

**SONG OF SONGS 2:17**
"Until the day breathes and the shadows flee, turn, my beloved, be like a gazelle or a young stag on cleft mountains."

## Inscribed upon My Heart

Use the Scripture memory verse for the week and the prayer prompt to bring your confession, thanksgiving, praise, and requests before the God who calls you beautiful.

### WEEK 2 MEMORY VERSE

"My beloved speaks and says to me: 'Arise, my love, my beautiful one, and come away, for behold, the winter is past; the rain is over and gone.'" Song of Songs 2:10–11

### PRAYER PROMPT

Father, we thank and praise You for the gift of Your Son and the glorious gift of relationship with You. Be in each of the relationships on my heart today, especially . . .

# Week 3

## WHAT ARE WE SEARCHING FOR?

# Viewer Guide

## VIDEO 3: DESIRE, DESPERATION, AND SALVATION
## SONG OF SONGS 3:1–3

**VERSES TO BOOKMARK**
Song of Songs 2:14–16
Song of Songs 5:6
Genesis 2:22–25
Genesis 3:16
Luke 7:36–48

Underline or circle each time you hear the words *sought* or *seek* or *found* in Song of Songs 3:1–3:

> On my bed by night
> I sought him whom my soul loves;
>     I sought him, but found him not.
> I will rise now and go about the city,
>     in the streets and in the squares;
> I will seek him whom my soul loves.
>     I sought him, but found him not.
> The watchmen found me
>     as they went about in the city.
> "Have you seen him whom my soul loves?"

## THREE CRITICAL INTERSECTIONS OF DESIRE

### 1. DESIRE AND CREATION

Our desires and longings in this life first point us to our _____.

We are _____ by God.

יְהֹוָה
*Yahweh*: LORD, the God who revealed Himself to Moses as the Great I AM.

Genesis 2:24–25: "Therefore a man shall leave his father and his mother and hold fast to his wife, and they shall become one flesh. And the man and his wife were both naked and were _____ _____."

## 2. Desire and Desperation in the Fall

Our desire becomes _____ in the fall.

Genesis 3:16: "To the woman He said, 'I will surely multiply your pain in childbearing; in pain you shall bring forth children. Your desire shall be

_____ _____ _____, and he shall

rule over you.'" (Another way to put it: "It shall be *toward* your husband.")

## Desire contrary to                    Desire toward/for

◄──────────────────────────────────────────►

Identity solely in self                                    Identity solely in others

Independence                                                            Dependence

Push away from any need                              Seek out protection
or longing for protection                                        and affection
and affection

Once sin entered the world, desire became sporadic, and we are now

desperate for _____.

## 3. Desire and Salvation

Because of this great state of _____ that sin has thrown us

into, we are now perfectly _____ for _____

_____. Our desire ultimately finds _____ in

Christ alone.

## Discussion Questions

1. Where have you seen desire well up in your own life?
2. Read through Ephesians 5:22–33. How is Christ the perfect fulfillment of all our desire? How does He perfectly represent the work of the head of the household?
3. Read Luke 7:36–48 again. How does Jesus honor the woman's desire? What does He offer her? What does He offer you in this account of Scripture?

# Day 1

SEARCHING FOR GOD
**SONG OF SONGS 3:1–4**

The Shulammite's desperation for Solomon in Song of Songs 3 mirrors our desperation for Jesus perfectly. Fill in the blanks below from the last video study. (If you need a cheat sheet, you can find the answers on p. 77.)

Because of this great _____ that sin has

thrown us into, we are now perfectly _____.

It's a good place to be—remembering the struggle that sin throws us into in this life, but appreciating all that God is doing with it through the work of Christ on the cross and His Spirit in our hearts and lives.

Look again at Song of Songs 3:3–4, and fill in the missing words below.

"The watchmen _____ me

as they went about in the city.

'Have you seen him whom my soul loves?'

Scarcely had I passed them when _____

_____ _____ whom my soul loves."

How does the Shulammite's search conclude?

Today, we are going to talk more about the kind of God who makes Himself found. Our God, in Christ, always comes to us first, seeks us first. We can't "find Him" on our own, but only by the Holy Spirit. It is really quite remarkable. Doesn't that just scream of great affection? I can rest easy; I am forgiven and loved in Christ.

This is good news to me. The part of life that seems so exhausting for me is all the searching. Egg hunts and scavenger hunts are fun when we're young, but as we grow up, those things can start to sound exhausting, and I truly believe it's because so much of life is taken up by searching:

- Searching for the right college or the right job

- The searching of young adulthood for who in the world you are

- Searching for an apartment or a house

- The searching of courtship and dating

- Searching for answers when confronted by difficult challenges

What else do people search for in life, literally or metaphorically?

What have been the most trying searches for you?

Even married life can feel like a game of hide-and-seek, constantly trying to discover more about who your husband is, what makes him tick, what interests him, and how you best fit together. Really, though, any deep personal relationships can feel this way. In every relationship, we have to figure out how to best communicate, the other person's likes and dislikes, and how to work through challenges together. While it's important not to play games (so maybe hide-and-seek isn't the best metaphor), it really is important to daily "find" each other, to seek each other out and dig a little deeper, draw a little closer. Marriage is fun and exhausting and wonderful, and I wouldn't trade it for the world.

Our God works differently from our earthly experiences and understandings. He is outside of the sin, misunderstandings, and heartache that sin brings. In dating, in friendships, in families, and in married life, we desire and pursue, but we are often disappointed because of expectations and the struggles of life that make our relationships less than what we desire.

Our God never disappoints. God shares who He is in His Word. He also specifically tells us all the ways He is found. He is never understood apart from His Word, but let's look more carefully at the ways in which He can be found, through the enlightening power of the Holy Spirit.

GOD IS FOUND IN THE NATURAL WORLD.

"For His invisible attributes, namely, His eternal power and divine nature, have been clearly perceived, ever since the creation of the world, in the things that have been made. So they are without excuse." Romans 1:20

God has gifted us with grass, trees, oceans, mountains, planets, and so much else that proclaims His majesty. When you look up at the stars, isn't it a wonder that we know the God of the universe? When you settle your feet in the sand and hear the roar of the waves, isn't it a wonder that the wind and waves obey Him? When you hear the birds sing their songs and the whales echo in the depths, do you believe that even they are made for His praise?

Look up the following passages about God's creation. What truths do you find about God being found in nature?

Isaiah 40:26

Job 38:11

Psalm 104

My favorite natural things include ocean waves, warm sunshine, flickering fire, the Great Lakes, and an autumn shower of leaves.

What is your favorite natural thing?

How does this thing reveal God's "power and divine nature"?

✝ GOD IS FOUND, INCARNATE, AS A MAN NAMED JESUS.

"The Word became flesh and made His dwelling among us. We have seen His glory, the glory of the one and only Son, who came from the Father, full of grace and truth." John 1:14 (NIV)

Our God is so far from hidden that He walked among us for thirty-three years. In the Old Testament, God instituted a sacrificial system to continuously point the people to the ultimate sacrifice that would end all sacrifices—Jesus Christ, our Savior. He was born in a manger, was baptized in the Jordan, ate with sinners like us, prayed in the garden, died on the cross, and walked out of the tomb. We can only find the truth about who Jesus is through God's Word, the Bible.

Philippians 2:8–11 tells us that Jesus was found in human form for what ultimate reason?

Take a moment for some praise and picture it: every tongue confessing and every knee bent before a God who makes Himself found.

 GOD IS FOUND THROUGH HIS PEOPLE.

"To the church of God that is in Corinth, to those sanctified in Christ Jesus, called to be saints together with all those who in every place call upon the name of our Lord Jesus Christ, both their Lord and ours: Grace to you and peace from God our Father and the Lord Jesus Christ. I give thanks to my God always for you because of the grace of God that was given you in Christ Jesus, that in every way you were enriched in Him in all speech and all knowledge—even as the testimony about Christ was confirmed among you." 1 Corinthians 1:2–6 (ESV)

Yep, God is found through you and me, and even the grouchy person at your church. God put Himself in us to be His witnesses to the world around us. He gave us His Word to gather around and bring encouragement to one another. The Word and the Spirit connect through His people to bring hope to a world in need.

Check out 2 Corinthians 3:2–3. What does God write on us for other people to see?

Our God is found in creation, in Jesus, and in His people. Which of these three ways is the most striking to you? Why?

Let's look to one more truth in His Word. Jeremiah 29:13 tells us:

> "You will seek Me and find Me when you search for Me with all your heart." (NASB)

Jesus really is the answer to absolutely everything. Luke 19:10 says:

> "For the Son of Man came to seek and to save the lost." (ESV)

 GOD FINDS US FIRST.

> "This is how God showed His love among us: He sent His one and only Son into the world that we might live through Him. This is love: not that we loved God, but that He loved us and sent His Son as an atoning sacrifice for our sins." 1 John 4:9–10 (NIV)

Before we even knew Him, God knew just who we are, just where we are, every pain in our heart, every sin, every need. We once were lost in our sin, but through Christ we are found. We might feel much like the Shulammite, searching and searching for her Beloved, but Baptism is the gift of the promise of eternity and knowing God intimately. It reminds us that we were found.

He has found us, and He allows Himself to be found. This is altogether beautiful.

## INSCRIBED UPON MY HEART

Use the Scripture memory verse for the week and the prayer prompt to bring your confession, thanksgiving, praise, and requests before the God who calls you beautiful.

### WEEK 3 MEMORY VERSE

"Scarcely had I passed them when I found him whom my soul loves." Song of Songs 3:4a

### PRAYER PROMPT

Jesus Christ, friend of sinners, You are the one my soul loves. Thank You for revealing Yourself in . . .

**ABOUT THIS VERSE**
Do not be mistaken; God finds us first, but He brings desire for Himself into our hearts and lives through the Holy Spirit—and we seek more of His Word and time with Him as we grow in Christ.

# Day 2

## SEARCHING IN DESPERATION
## SONG OF SONGS 3:4–5

I once spent a week with twenty-two eighth graders, touring Washington, DC. We walked forty-four miles in five days, according to my friend's fitness tracker. We saw monuments and museums, ate in food courts filled to bursting, and rode around town in our chariot . . . ahem . . . giant charter bus. The streets were filled to overflowing with thirteen-year-olds. We descended on Washington, DC, the very week that every other eighth-grade class in the country also visited DC. Everywhere we went, everywhere I looked, there were eighth graders. My "poor behavior" alarm was on full alert.

I expected rowdy and ridiculous.

I expected loud.

I expected disrespectful.

I expected annoyance and frustration.

Instead what I got was shockingly wonderful. I didn't expect to have the enjoyable time I had. I didn't expect to be impressed with eighth graders. I didn't expect to miss their joyous and rambunctious laughter when we all went back to our normal lives.

My expectations had fooled me. I had expected so little of them. And why? Because they were thirteen? Because they were young? There are whole Scripture verses that speak of my error! (I apologize eighth graders, and I'm glad you proved me wrong!)

**1 TIMOTHY 4:12**
"Let no one despise you for your youth, but set the believers an example in speech, in conduct, in love, in faith, in purity."

Like my low expectations for the eighth graders, what low expectations do you have?

How often do we hold low expectations in our relationship with God? How often do we settle for "okay" and "just enough" instead of thriving, growing, and drawing near? How often do we settle for ho-hum Christianity when God offers the power of His Spirit and growth in our hearts and lives?

Mark on the line below where you are in your faith walk during this season of life. Be honest; there is no intended judgment here, just recognition.

Ho-Hum                                                                    Drawing
Relationship                                                     Nearer Every
with God                                                                      Day

_____

We discussed in our video the desperation that comes as a result of our separation from God in the fall into sin. We also discussed how God uses that desperation to point us toward His great love for us and His salvation for us. While desperation sounds like something we'd like to push far, far away, maybe we need to change up our expectations.

# MAYBE IT'S TIME FOR US TO EMBRACE DESPERATE.

The Shulammite was desperate for her beloved because she feared losing him. She feared being anywhere he was not.

Read Song of Songs 3:4–5. When the Shulammite finds Solomon, what is her reaction?

When you lose something, you're much more likely to hold on more tightly to it once it is found. Sometimes, desperation is just what we need. C. S. Lewis once wrote:

> If we consider the unblushing promise of reward and the staggering nature of rewards promised in the Gospels, it would seem that our Lord finds our desires not too strong, but too weak. We are halfhearted creatures, fooling about with drink and sex and ambition when infinite joy is offered us, like an ignorant child who wants to go on making mud pies in a slum because he can not imagine what is meant by the offer of a holiday at sea. We are far too easily pleased.[25]

What are some ways in which you are "far too easily pleased" in your faith walk?

Some growth seasons of our lives look more like desperation. Desperation usually doesn't feel awesome. It doesn't usually even feel good. In fact, often it feels like we're lost, scared, sad, or all of the above. But if that's what leads us closer to Christ, maybe sometimes we need to say, "So be it." While we don't need to be desperate, because Christ is always there, always faithful, it can be a good thing, a growth thing.

# CHRIST DOES BEAUTIFUL THINGS IN DESPERATE PEOPLE.

**DESPERATE**
When everything else we have tried has failed, when we're at the end of our rope, when we don't know what else to do . . . a perfect place to be for God to do His work.

Mary Magdalene knew about desperation. Read an account from her story in John 20:1–17. What was Mary searching for in this passage?

What phrases or actions in the passage give you the sense that Mary was desperate?

Mary, just like the Shulammite, is the beloved searching for the one whom her soul loves, who is Christ. It doesn't have to be romantic love to be desperate love. In fact, I think Spirit-filled love is more desperate for the object of its affection than any romantic love ever could be, because one is built on selfishness and the other on pure Gospel. Mary genuinely cannot imagine life apart from her Savior, Jesus. Desperation of this variety, a desperation rooted in who Christ is and what He does for us, pours out in love of God and neighbor rather than love of self that asks, "What can I get out of this?"

The Bible is full of accounts of people desperate to draw closer to God. Jot down any you can think of in the space below. (For some hints, check out Psalm 63, Job 7, Genesis 18, and Philippians 1.)

The Jewish people entered a time of silence from God during the four hundred years between the Old and New Testaments. No doubt it was a difficult test of faith for them. We will never know a silent God. We have been given the gift of His Word instead of silence. The Holy Spirit worked through men who wrote on scrolls and pages the words of our God so that we could draw near to our Savior. In this Word, the Book of Hebrews (ESV) uses the phrase "draw [or drawing] near" seven times! Hebrews 4:15–16 is by far my favorite.

What does God offer us in His Word according to Hebrews 4:15–16?

What verses in Scripture do you return to time and again to find food for your soul?

For me, hymns often calm my heart during times when I don't know where to look in my desperation. The music speaks God's truth and allows the prayer to rise to the surface from deep in my heart, sometimes out of nowhere. Look through the words of "I Am Trusting Thee, Lord Jesus" below, and circle anything listed that we can trust Jesus for in our moments of confidence and our moments of desperation.

### I Am Trusting Thee, Lord Jesus[26]
(*LSB* 729)

I am trusting Thee, Lord Jesus,
Trusting only Thee;
Trusting Thee for full salvation,
Great and free.

I am trusting Thee for pardon;
At Thy feet I bow,
For Thy grace and tender mercy
Trusting now.

I am trusting Thee for cleansing
In the crimson flood;
Trusting Thee to make me holy
By Thy blood.

I am trusting Thee to guide me;
Thou alone shalt lead,
Ev'ry day and hour supplying
All my need.

I am trusting Thee for power;
Thine can never fail.
Words which Thou Thyself shalt give me
Must prevail.

I am trusting Thee, Lord Jesus;
Never let me fall.
I am trusting Thee forever
And for all.

What comfort!

God invites us to draw near to Him and to His Word. And when we grab tightly to that invitation with the help of the Holy Spirit, something happens . . . we can't get enough. We become desperate for more God and less of ourselves (John 3:30). We are fed and filled in our desperation through His Word and His Spirit.

Beloved, draw near to Him. His mercy and grace reach down to you, whether you're desperate or ho-hum. As always, He is altogether beautiful.

## Inscribed upon My Heart

Use the Scripture memory verse for the week and the prayer prompt to bring your confession, thanksgiving, praise, and requests before the God who calls you beautiful.

### WEEK 3 MEMORY VERSE

"Scarcely had I passed them when I found him whom my soul loves." Song of Songs 3:4a

### PRAYER PROMPT

Holy Spirit, guide my path with the word of truth. Today I need your help to . . .

# Lord, I Need You[27]

Lord, I come, I confess
Bowing here I find my rest
Without You I fall apart
You're the one that guides my heart

Lord, I need You, oh, I need You
Every hour I need You
My one defense, my righteousness
Oh God, how I need You

Where sin runs deep Your
    grace is more
Where grace is found is where
    You are
And where You are, Lord, I am free
Holiness is Christ in me

Lord, I need You, oh, I need You
Every hour I need You
My one defense, my righteousness
Oh God, how I need You
To teach my song to rise to You

When temptation comes my way
When I cannot stand I'll fall on You
Jesus, You're my hope and stay
Lord, I need You, oh, I need You
Every hour I need You

My one defense, my righteousness
Oh God, how I need You
You're my one defense, my righteousness
Oh God, how I need You
My one defense, my righteousness

—MATT MAHER

"Let us then with confidence draw near to the throne of grace, that we may receive mercy and find grace to help in time of need."

Hebrews 4:16

# Day 3

## SEARCHING FOR CONSUMMATION
## SONG OF SONGS 3:6–11

In Song of Songs 3:6–11, we are blessed to attend a wedding. This one is the stuff of dreams. And if you're anything like me, you're anxious for the wedding details. I love to know the colors, the location, the songs, and the stories shared, but those details of this particular wedding we'll save for to-morrow. For today's study, we're going to focus on the movement of the story in chapter 3—the story of Christ and His Bride, the Church, told through the story of the Shulammite and her Lover.

As we read through chapter 3, we get to see the work of God across all of history within a single chapter of Scripture. Theologically, the chapter moves something like this:

> God moves from the hidden God (vv. 1–3)
>
> to the revealed, incarnate God (vv. 4–5)
>
> to the consummate God (vv. 6–11).

This is one place in the Song where we can very clearly see the allegory within the historic narrative, and it follows the threefold path outlined above. The epic that is eternity began before creation and continues beyond Christ's return for us. In that epic, God moves from more hidden to less hidden as He reveals Himself in Christ, reveals Himself more in His Word, and then reveals Himself completely when He comes back for us. Because of this revealing over time, there are still parts of Him and His plan that we do not completely see or understand.

Use the three titles "hidden God," "revealed God," and "consummate God" to fill in the blanks below.

There was a time for God to remain hidden. In Old Testament times, God

was a _____.

There was a time for God to reveal Himself in the person of Christ. In the

New Testament, God was a _____.

There will be a time for the restoration of the whole creation and the wedding feast of the Lamb. In that time, in the restoration, God will be a

_____.

Now, let's dig into this deeper.

## THE HIDDEN GOD—GOD AND MAN BEFORE CHRIST JESUS

From the Old Testament we know that God, in Trinity, created the universe. Read the first part of Genesis 1:26 below, and circle the pronouns in the verse.

"Then God said, 'Let Us make man in Our image, after Our likeness.'"

The little words *Us* and *Our* are a great and awesome way that God begins to reveal Himself from the very beginning. This seemingly tiny revealing is like a big present with multiple layers of wrapping paper. When Christ comes back to reign in the new creation, we will see the full present unveiled. Moses is the writer of these words in Genesis. I wonder what Moses understood of God's eternal plan when he first penned Genesis, inspired by the Spirit.

Over time, God instituted the sacrificial system as a way for His people to come to Him and meet with Him. What does Leviticus 17:11 tell us the sacrifices were for?

Through the Old Testament sacrifices, God gave man a way to experience the assurance of forgiveness in his sinful state. But He kept the person of Christ, the work of Christ, hidden for revealing at just the right time. God did not withhold Himself from His people, but can you see how His nature was more hidden before the incarnation of Jesus? He did reveal His plan to people in His time, in His way. The people of the Old Testament waited and hungered for God to show pieces of Himself through the words of the prophets. God also revealed Himself through the nation of Israel, as a people set apart, to show His mighty works to the surrounding nations.

## THE REVEALED GOD IN CHRIST

Jesus changes everything. John 1:14 calls Him the Word who "dwelt among us." In Jesus, God's message of salvation has come down to earth to reveal God's plan for saving His people. Christ's mediation on behalf of all people changes our relationship with God.

Read John 15:15. What did God once call us, before Christ's incarnation, death, and resurrection? What does God call us now?

How does this relational change impact you personally? What is different about a master's relationship with a servant and the relationship between two friends?

The promise of God to us is that everyone is given the opportunity to believe in the Lord Jesus Christ and be saved. Read each of the Scripture texts below. Next to each reference, write whom God has revealed Himself to and how.

Romans 16:25–27

Colossians 1:24–28

**Colossians 1:27**
"To them God chose to make known how great among the Gentiles are the riches of the glory of this mystery, *which is Christ in you, the hope of glory*" (emphasis added).

1 Corinthians 2:8–12

To Jew and Gentile, slave and free, male and female—everyone—God reveals Himself in Christ, so that every single one of us has the opportunity to come to Him.

## THE CONSUMMATE GOD

While we know God both through the person of Christ, His death, and resurrection and through the work of His Spirit living in us, there will yet be a time when we will *fully* know God in a way we can't even imagine. And that time will come when He comes back for us. Today, we are now-and-not-yet people. God is revealed to us, but we wait for the fullness of time, that wedding feast of Christ and His Bride, at His return.

This brings us back to our Shulammite woman in Song of Songs 3. She knows her Beloved, but she wakes in the night and searches for him, desiring the time when she will fully know him at the consummation of their marriage and in their married life together. As part of the Church on earth, we, too, wait for consummation with our Lord and Savior, when we will fully be with Him, face-to-face.

One day, it will be time for a wedding like no eye has seen!

What do each of the following passages tell us about the consummation of Christ and His Bride, the Church—that glorious time when Jesus comes back again for us? I did the first one to get you started.

Luke 8:17 *Nothing is hidden that we will not eventually know; one day God will reveal the entire picture to us.*

> **LUKE 8:17**
> "For nothing is hidden that will not become evident, nor anything secret that will not be known and come to light." (NASB)

Revelation 19:7–9

Ephesians 5:25–27

Mark 13:32

Revelation 22:17

> **REVELATION 22:17**
> "The Spirit and the Bride say, 'Come.' And let the one who hears say, 'Come.' And let the one who is thirsty come; let the one who desires take the water of life without price."

We live in the now-and-not-yet. We know the hidden God who was revealed to us in Christ Jesus. We stand in a time of waiting, for a wedding feast like no other. Isn't it altogether beautiful?

# INSCRIBED UPON MY HEART

How are you doing with the Scripture memory verse for the week? Utilize the verse for the week and the prayer prompt to bring your confession, thanksgiving, praise, and requests before the God who calls you beautiful.

## WEEK 3 MEMORY VERSE

"Scarcely had I passed them when I found him whom my soul loves." Song of Songs 3:4a

## PRAYER PROMPT

Father, thank You for revealing Jesus to me . . .

# Day 4

## SEARCHING FOR GLADNESS
## SONG OF SONGS 3:6–11

It's time for wedding details! I love being a part of wedding celebrations. When one of our young adults from church was married, I couldn't wait to watch her walk down the aisle. I have known this precious girl since she was eight years old. I have watched her grow in faith and life and love. Her wedding was scheduled for the day before I was to return from a trip with my daughter. It was a meeting of the most unfortunate timing, but such is life. I had to miss the wedding, but you had better believe I wanted details. I returned from my trip and immediately poked and prodded my husband about colors and textures and special moments and smiles and sparkles. I wanted to know it all. My husband eventually wore thin on this kind of talk and encouraged me to have lunch with the bride to rehash all the juicy snippets.

Song of Songs 3:6–11 is wedding details at its best. We get a roadside seat to Solomon's entourage coming for his bride on their wedding day. Solomon had wealth such as the world had never seen, and from the sound of it, he took advantage of his resources to make his wedding day to the Shulammite woman grand. After studying about the Beloved's search for her groom, isn't it fantastic to hear the story of him coming for her?

Read Song of Songs 3:6–11. As you read, note the elements of lavishness that stick out to you. Tap into your sensory system and list each rich element next to one of the five senses below.

Taste

Sight

Smell

Hearing

Touch

These are some of my favorite types of Scripture verses, the ones that make you feel like you are there, attending the event. The poetic and vivid language of the book helps us to slip in and soak up every moment of the festivities. But we aren't crashing the wedding—we are actually invited! That is the way the Bible is designed; it's an invitation to meet with God and hear from Him in every verse.

In Song of Songs 3:6–7, who joins Solomon's *litter*?

As Solomon processes with his mighty men to claim his bride, Christ desires to claim His Bride, the Church. We are the Church—you and me, all believers in Christ Jesus, the saints around us and the saints who have gone before us. We are not the onlookers on the side of the road in this passage or the mighty men supporting Solomon's wealth and greatness. *We are the Bride* for whom the Lover comes!

This is our wedding.

The King spares no expense, not even the life of His one and only Son, so that we, His people, may be united with Him. Think of the pomp and circumstance of royal weddings in our world today. These lavish affairs probably do not even hold a candle to Solomon's procession for his wedding to the Shulammite that day. And no wedding can even begin to compare with the wealth and grace of the marriage feast of the Lamb. When Christ comes back for His Bride, God, who designs and orders all of creation, will prepare a wedding feast that far surpasses all wedding feasts.

Let's highlight a few of the metaphorical images in Song of Songs 3:6–7 that point us to the deeper meaning beyond Solomon's story, to that greater type of Christ and His Bride.

 SONG OF SONGS 3:6: "MYRRH AND FRANKINCENSE"

These scents are part of the Gospel accounts of both Christ's birth and His death and resurrection.

Read the following passages and note the purposes for which myrrh and frankincense were used in each circumstance.

Matthew 2:1–2, 10–11

John 19:38–40

## ⚔ Song of Songs 3:8: "Each with his sword at his thigh, against terror by night"

The men in the wedding procession come bearing swords. Their wartime training is an asset to the wedding party. How strange to think of that!

What would the mighty men need to defend against during the wedding procession?

Roads can be dangerous places; shining your wealth before the world can attract all kinds of problems. When we shine the light of Christ, which dwells inside His people, we also will attract trouble of various kinds from this world, which is opposed to Him.

What trouble might befall a traveler with some obvious wealth, in Solomon's time and in our time today?

What other troubles do we encounter in this life?

John 10:10–12 reminds us of what Satan is trying to do as a robber and thief in our lives. How does Satan try to steal our peace, our joy, our light from us?

Thieves, robbers, and troublemakers didn't stop Solomon from being lavish when he came for his bride. In the same way, we should not be deterred from being lavish in sharing the love of God and joy of the Holy Spirit. Solomon was well equipped with mighty protection. We are well equipped by a mighty God. We have the protection of God's promise of eternity.

Write out John 10:11 below, as a reminder of this promise of protection.

When in your life has God offered His strength and the knowledge of His salvation to protect your soul?

 SONG OF SONGS 3:10: "ITS SEAT OF PURPLE"

This is such a small detail, but doesn't purple just sound like a wedding color? It is also the color attributed to wealth and royalty throughout the Bible.

During the season of Lent, many churches use purple cloths as drapes on the altar or as other adornments. Why might this be? Read Revelation 1:4–5 and 19:16, and list the names for Jesus.

Jesus stepped down from His throne in heaven to bring salvation to us. He is no less a King while hanging on a shabby cross than He is at His triumphant return. The purple at Lent reminds us that His blood was given and shed for you. You are loved by the King of the universe. Take a moment to let that reality soak in.

 SONG OF SONGS 3:11: "ON THE DAY OF THE GLADNESS OF HIS HEART"

If you would be so kind, share something or someone in life that makes your heart swell. What makes your heart glad?

You make God's heart glad. In 1 John 3:1, we are told of God's extravagant love for us in Christ Jesus. You can't beat the NIV translation for this one:

"See what great love the Father has lavished on us, that we should be called children of God! And that is what we are! The reason the world does not know us is that it did not know Him." (NIV)

I'm a sucker for exclamation points, and this passage certainly deserves a couple. We are children of the Most High God. He rides His horse and chariot to claim us as His own. All praise to Him! I cannot wait for the day we see Him face-to-face. That will surely be

δίδωμι
*didomi*: give, pour, offer, grant, bestow

## "the day of the gladness of His heart." Song of Songs 3:11

We are claimed by a Groom who lavishly loves His Bride. That is altogether beautiful.

### INSCRIBED UPON MY HEART

Use the Scripture memory verse for the week and the prayer prompt to bring your confession, thanksgiving, praise, and requests before the God who calls you beautiful.

### WEEK 3 MEMORY WORK

"Scarcely had I passed them when I found him whom my soul loves." Song of Songs 3:4a

### PRAYER PROMPT

Jesus, You are King of kings and worthy of praise and honor . . .

# Day 5

Once upon a time, Dave and Heidi Goehmann were married. Before that day, my husband and I had many an argument about who and who not to invite to the wedding. In my mind, only the likes of Hollywood can afford endless food and drink for an untold amount of guests. My husband, however, takes very seriously Jesus' words in Luke 14:13, and it's hard to argue when he is so cute and has the Bible on his side. He won, and we invited *everyone*. There were open invitations in various church bulletins. If you regularly served us in a restaurant, you got an invite, and if we happened to run into you in the store the week before the wedding, you were invited as well. My husband vowed no one would feel poor in spirit by being left out of our wedding celebration. It's something I absolutely love about him to this day.

The story is well-known in our families. We had so many people at our wedding feast that we almost ran out of food, but (and here's where it gets really cool) the food lasted until every last guest was served. My husband and I got the last three meatballs and two bites of cheese. We didn't get to eat a piece of our own wedding cake, but we couldn't have cared less. We were filled to the brim with happiness, love, and the sight of so many smiling faces to share it with. I was floored by the people who drove from near and far to share the day with us, and it wouldn't have been complete without each and every one of them.

Song of Songs 3:11 includes a very special wedding guest. Please read this passage and note who the guest is.

The groom's mother, in our culture, is a background character at most weddings. She holds a supporting role, but the unspoken truth is that her primary job is to not steal any glory from the bride, or the bride's mom, or any other woman at the wedding. The same is not true for the wedding of King Solomon and his bride. This groom's mother is held in a place of honor.

When we remind ourselves who this woman is, we might even be a little more surprised. Scan back to our very first day of study and remind yourself who Solomon's mother is. Write her name below.

Perhaps no Bible account is more familiar to us when we hear this name than that of David and Bathsheba's adultery. We try to package it in ways even the smallest of children can hear, because it very clearly demonstrates the consequences of sin. The consequences in this particular instance are found in 2 Samuel 12. But God, in His mercy and grace, does not allow those consequences to rule in David and Bathsheba's lives. Solomon is born as the second child to this notorious couple.

You see, God does not allow our sin to define us. That is not in His character. The world may use our sins to label us: adulterer, thief, mistake, impostor. But God tells us a different truth. Through Christ, there is forgiveness—and a new identity.

Look up each of the following passages, and write down the truth about our sin revealed in each one.

Psalm 103:11–12

> **IDENTITY**
> Who or what a person or thing is. As believers, we reserve this for who we are in Christ Jesus alone.

Isaiah 1:18

Romans 8:38–39

And so Bathsheba also is not defined by the sin she committed with King David. Instead, God speaks love and forgiveness over her, and through the covering of sacrifices that point to the Messiah to come in the grand plan of God, God bestows on her honor. On the great and grand wedding day of her son Solomon, this is clear for all to see. She is given the startling honor of not only having a place of honor at her son's wedding but also of being intimately involved with Solomon's calling as king.

How often is it *grace* that needs to be invited to the party, for ourselves and as a gift we bestow on other people?

There is more to the story than meets the eye. Turn to 1 Kings 1:11–31. How did God use Bathsheba and the prophet Nathan to bring Solomon to the throne as king?

Remember that Nathan was the one to confront David about his sin with Bathsheba. Nathan was not only David's friend but also the whistle-blower sent by God to uncover the truth of David and Bathsheba's relationship. In 1 Kings 11, we are shown that when God offers forgiveness, full and free, He means it. God's forgiveness, offered by the prophet Nathan, is thorough and not weighed down by shoulda-coulda-woulda. Nathan comes to Bathsheba with a posture of care for her in 1 Kings 1.

Write Nathan's words to Bathsheba in 1 Kings 1:12 below.

The uncovering of sin does not bring death; it brings life. Nathan, although intimately acquainted with Bathsheba's sin, is concerned for her life. Similarly, God sends us His word of conviction because He cares, because His wish is to restore each of His children to Himself. God uses people like Nathan in our own lives to bring us grace.

Who has been a "Nathan" in your life—someone who will point out a sin, hear your confession, and share God's grace with you?

If you have a specific time when someone helped you to turn from sin and experience God's grace, please share it, vaguely or specifically.

**FUN FACT**
In Scripture, *Zion* (as in "daughters of Zion," Song of Songs 3:11) usually refers to the Temple Mount in Jerusalem, where God dwelt among His people in the Old Testament. Metaphorically, Zion can include all of Israel or all of God's people throughout eternity (*TLSB*, p. 844).

In Song of Songs 3:11, we see Bathsheba's part in the gladness of her treasured son's heart, bestowing a crown on him "on the day of his wedding." She is not just a guest but an honored guest at a wedding to remember. We will let people down in our lives, and people will let us down. We will encounter Nathans who encourage us and we will be a Nathan to someone else. In all of it, God will do His work, through the grace of His Son.

Where else in life does grace need to be invited to the party? What was a situation recently where you can look back and say, "Grace would have been better there"?

What value does confession and absolution—forgiveness—have in relationships? In what ways can we share it in our everyday interactions?

God gives us the mirror of the Law to see our sin, so that we can experience the same Gospel grace Bathsheba was given. This work of this Law and Gospel in our daily lives is altogether beautiful.

## INSCRIBED UPON MY HEART

Use the Scripture memory verse for the week and the prayer prompt to bring your confession, thanksgiving, praise, and requests before the God who calls you beautiful.

### WEEK 3 MEMORY VERSE

"Scarcely had I passed them when I found him whom my soul loves" Song of Songs 3:4a

### PRAYER PROMPT

Father, Savior, and Spirit, Your truth and Your forgiveness is life and salvation . . .

# A Man's Take on Song of Songs 3

The Song of Songs may not feel like a manly book, but in my mind, there is great appeal for men here. Images representing the Beloved as a stag or a gazelle make me think of strength and speed, and the fact that the stag stands with such strength and confidence—what every man wishes he could do in his life. Yes, the Song of Songs is full of poetry and imagery that might seem like a girl's dream for her man, but these dreams the Shulammite bride has for her husband make me drift into a fantasy of my own where I alone am the central figure. I almost can't help but swell up with the idea that she is talking about me.

Many men, I presume, want to identify with the Beloved, to be seen like Solomon, strong and powerful. And while the Shulammite speaks of the outward appearance of her Beloved, my thoughts draw me to contemplate my desire for internal strength and power. Who wouldn't desire to be strong, confident, and solid? Most single men would probably love to be seen as strong and able like Solomon. As a married man, I, too, want to be seen as a protector and provider, particularly for my wife and family.

In my younger years, I had puffed-up fantasies that I thought could more or less come true. As a husband of seventeen years, my inflated ego is crushed with reality. For instance, I'm certainly bad at the whole romantic thing. I don't think of very creative dates. I don't think I've ever surprised my wife with a getaway weekend. I always thought I would be the manly hunter who could bring home a trophy buck, and instead I brought home a small doe. Instead of leaping like a gazelle, I once pulled my hamstring playing softball and gave up playing. I would suspect that no matter how much we fantasize, a man notices that deep down he is not so strong, not so confident.

The result of recognizing all my failures, though, is that it shifts my thoughts to the one who is perfect: to my Savior, Jesus Christ. It is not so much that I love Him like the Bride loves the Beloved in the text. It is more that Christ can do what I cannot. Christ is the hero who got the girl (the whole Church!). He alone deserves all the glory. He is the King of kings, the Lord of lords, majestic, honorable, noble, worthy.

At the end of the day, if we are inclined to reflect on Christ, the Song of Songs has pointed us in the right direction. We see an incredible description of the strong, confident Christ, who did beat Satan—the fox that tries to spoil all our vineyards, our families, our lives. Christ is the perfect man whose death was the perfect sacrifice for humanity. That is the message of strength and beauty for both men and women in this epic love story.

—*PASTOR DAVID GOEHMANN*
Husband, father, bowhunter, redeemed by Christ

# Week 4

## BUT AM I REALLY BEAUTIFUL?

# Viewer Guide

## VIDEO 4: ALTOGETHER BEAUTIFUL
## SONG OF SONGS 4:1–7

**VERSES TO BOOKMARK**
Song of Songs 4:1-7
John 8:44
Isaiah 3:16–17, 24
Mark 14:6

**ABOUT THIS PASSAGE**
Don't you wish someone complimented your teeth or your cheeks more? This passage is a good reminder that the poetry of the Song of Songs was written in a different time and place from our own. Still, we hear God's love for each of us and for His Church in these verses. He sees altogether beautiful when He looks on us.

God is concerned with the concept of _____.

Note or underline every reference to physical beauty you find in Song of Songs 4:1–7:

Behold, you are beautiful, my love,

   behold, you are beautiful!

Your eyes are doves

   behind your veil.

Your hair is like a flock of goats

   leaping down the slopes of Gilead.

Your teeth are like a flock of shorn ewes

   that have come up from the washing,

all of which bear twins,

   and not one among them has lost its young.

Your lips are like a scarlet thread,

   and your mouth is lovely.

Your cheeks are like halves of a pomegranate

behind your veil.

Your neck is like the tower of David,

   built in rows of stone;

on it hang a thousand shields,

   all of them shields of warriors.

Your two breasts are like two fawns,

   twins of a gazelle,

   that graze among the lilies.

Until the day breathes

   and the shadows flee,

I will go away to the mountain of myrrh

   and the hill of frankincense.

You are altogether beautiful, my love;

   there is no flaw in you.

# Two Kinds of Beauty Addressed in the Bible

## 1. Deceptive Beauty

It is _____.

It is _____. Deceptive beauty is something that can be bought

and traded in the marketplace.

It is _____.

## 2. Authentic Beauty

It is related to _____.

It is _____.

> **1 Peter 3:3–4**
> "Do not let your adorning be external—the braiding of hair and the putting on of gold jewelry, or the clothing you wear—but let your adorning be the hidden person of the heart with the imperishable beauty of a gentle and quiet spirit, which in God's sight is very precious."

Mark 14:6: "But Jesus said, 'Leave her alone. Why do you trouble her? She

has done a _____ _____ to Me.'"

It is _____.

It isn't tied to _____. It's tied to _____.

When God looks at us, He sees two things: His beautiful _____

and His beautiful _____.

## Discussion Questions

1. Where do you see the economic aspects of beauty in our world today?

2. What is one thing you discerned today about your own physical beauty?

3. What is one thing you can encourage another woman with regarding her physical beauty?

# Day 1

YOU ARE BEAUTIFUL
SONG OF SONGS 4:1–7

I have a long and complicated history of trying to be at home in my body. I struggle with my body image like a tennis match. One day I feel pretty, and the next I berate myself for chubby curves and unruly hair. The bigger problem is that my body image issues are not my own. I share them with my daughter, with my sisters, with my friends, with the other moms in the school pickup line, and with the women in my churches.

I would like to think that my body image issues are mine and mine alone, but I have noticed something: every time I use humor to cut down my body, every time I beg off a compliment as untrue, every time I ask my husband "Does this make me look fat? frumpy? ugly?" I impact not only myself but the watchers and listeners. At fifteen years old, my daughter has already begun to disparage her body's imperfections. I can hear her friends disparage their own. I am not the only mom at the potluck feeling guilty about the one cookie I'm eating that day or the sugar in the punch or the cheese slice I consumed. While our culture does have a critical issue with excess, we also have a critical issue with "I'm not good enough, smart enough, pretty enough, funny enough. I'm not enough."

Body image is also a community issue. I need to consider my influence on many people beyond my four walls. God did not make us little islands. He made us to be connected people. This may be most evident to those of us who are plugged in to a great church community. What would your life be like without the community of believers that surrounds you? What would life be like without those people to share the dark storms and the triumphs of life?

How can I cut down my own body, a body created and gifted to me by a loving Father, and expect the person sitting next to me to fall in love with her own? You and I are part of this great cloud of witnesses and a tribe we could call Fearless Women, Children of God, Redeemed and Set Free. Today, we are going to settle in to Song of Songs 4 and become firmly grounded in what God says is beautiful about me, about you, about each of us.

If you were able to get in the video study this week, you found out a little more about how Scripture defines beauty. It was enlightening to me to understand that God does not devalue physical beauty, but that authentic—real and true—beauty is seated with His creation and redemption in mind. I am beautiful as His creation. I am flawless in His salvation.

In Song of Songs 4:1–7, we see the beloved bride standing before Solomon on their wedding day. Can you picture them standing across from each other? What is the groom's assessment of the bride? Below, list each of her features that he compliments in these seven verses.

Several commentators point out the familiarity with which Solomon extols his bride. Matthew Henry states:

> He does not flatter her, nor design hereby either to make her proud of herself or to court her praises of him; but, It is to encourage her under her present dejections. Whatever others thought of her, she was amiable in his eyes.[28]

Solomon states the truth he sees in her to build her up. There is no flattery or manipulation involved in his words, just truth spoken in love.

What kind of compliments can you offer others about their physical appearance to build them up? Share a specific person and compliment you can give. If you have the time and energy, list two or three people and compliments that you might share with them.

How do these compliments differ from flattery?

There are those in our lives whose opinions matter. Then there are others whose opinions should not bear weight in our lives. Solomon wanted his bride to know that she was beautiful *in his eyes*, as God created her. She was complete for him. If you look at Song of Songs 4:1–7, you may notice it is a holistic passage, identifying the beautiful features of the Shulammite from the top of her head down to her midsection. (This is complemented by Song of Songs 7, when the compliments travel from bottom to top.) The passage is neatly sandwiched together between verses 1 and 7. Look at these two verses again.

"Behold, you are beautiful, my love."

"You are altogether beautiful, my love."

*She is altogether beautiful*. God knit her together in a way that all of her parts lend to the glory of one another. The bride is *entirely* beautiful to her groom, as a whole person. She is a gift from God, the creator and sustainer of all things, as we proclaim Him in the Apostles' Creed, Maker of heaven and earth.[29] He made us altogether beautiful, redeems us beautiful in Christ, and sends His Spirit to beautify, or sanctify, our hearts and minds. (See p. 115 for the Apostles' Creed in its entirety and a bit of backstory on this historic creed.)

Tomorrow, we'll delve into how Song of Songs 4:1–7 also applies to Christ's Bride, the Church, but for now, let's keep these verses very personal.

Similar to Song of Songs 4:1–7, Psalm 139:13–15 proclaims that we are altogether wonderfully made, in all our parts.

Please read Psalm 139:13–15 below, and underline any descriptive adjectives you find about God's creation of every tiny little human ever made, including you.

"For You formed my inward parts;
    You knitted me together in my mother's womb.
I praise You, for I am fearfully and wonderfully made.
Wonderful are Your works;
    my soul knows it very well.
My frame was not hidden from You,
    when I was being made in secret,
    intricately woven in the depths of the earth."

God looks on us, as Solomon looked on his bride, and says, "You are My complete and wonderful creation. Each part, each intricate piece of you, is formed by Me" (Heidi's paraphrase).

Let's celebrate that! Below I've listed the features of the Shulammite's body that Solomon compliments throughout the entire chapter of Song of Songs 4. Look at my list and circle the feature that you most often struggle to believe is beautiful on your own body. Answer the following question beside the part you chose.

Why is it difficult for you to believe this part is beautiful?

Eyes

Hair

Teeth


Lips


Cheeks/Face


Neck


Breasts/Torso


If this exercise was extra helpful, choose two or three more parts to do.

Now, cross out the thoughts you wrote beside each of those parts. If you have a bold-colored marker, use it! Next to each and every part, write the words "altogether beautiful."

This exercise might seem tedious or even futile, but it helps us to rewrite the truth in our minds. God calls us altogether beautiful. It may not instantly change the way we feel about our noses or our hips or our unruly hair, but standing in truth is never in vain. The Word, written in Scripture, goes into our hearts and settles deep down in the secret places.

Can you do me a favor and write below one part of your body that you are pleased with? Just one part—you can do this!

Our Creator God makes each of us unique and truly wonderful. It is not our job to conform to anyone's standards, but simply to take care of the unique creation He has given us. In today's prayer prompt, take the opportunity to praise Him for what He has done as He knit and wove every single part of you. He deems you beautiful as His creation. He believes it, and so should we. Also remember that you stand flawless before God in the fullest sense because of the work of Christ Jesus, your Redeemer. May the Spirit fill you with awe and wonder at His marvelous work!

# Inscribed upon My Heart

Use the Scripture memory verse for the week and the prayer prompt to bring your confession, thanksgiving, praise, and requests before the God who calls you beautiful.

**ABOUT THIS VERSE**
God made us with His own hands. He knit us in our mother's womb. He proclaims His children the crown of His creation, *very* good. Through Christ Jesus and the forgiveness He offers us, God the Father sees us through the lens of grace and calls us flawless, altogether beautiful.

## WEEK 4 MEMORY VERSE

"You are altogether beautiful, my love; there is no flaw in you." Song of Songs 4:7

## PRAYER PROMPT

Father, thank You for making and forming me. Thank You for Your attention to detail and Your tender heart toward each of us . . .

# The Apostles' Creed

### THE FIRST ARTICLE

I believe in God, the Father Almighty,
Maker of heaven and earth.

### THE SECOND ARTICLE

And in Jesus Christ, His only Son, our Lord, who was conceived by the Holy Spirit, born of the Virgin Mary, suffered under Pontius Pilate, was crucified, died and was buried. He descended into hell. The third day He rose again from the dead. He ascended into heaven and sits at the right hand of God, the Father Almighty. From thence He will come to judge the living and the dead.

### THE THIRD ARTICLE

I believe in the Holy Spirit, the holy Christian church, the communion of saints, the forgiveness of sins, the resurrection of the body, and the life everlasting. Amen.

The origin of the Apostles' Creed isn't entirely clear, but it has been known to be in existence and in use by the Church since the late fourth century AD. The blessing of the Apostles' Creed is that it is a very concise and clear testament to the beliefs of the Church. It is a helpful way for believers to profess regularly their common beliefs in the triune God, Christ as Savior, original sin, the divine and human natures of Christ as Lord, the resurrection of the dead, and many other commonalities across Christian denominations.

# Day 2

## THE BODY IS BEAUTIFUL
### SONG OF SONGS 4:1–7

Ephesians 5 proclaims that Christ will one day present His Bride, the Church, without blemish or stain, without so much as a wrinkle in her white robe. Does this concept seem unrealistic to you? Churches are definitely not perfect. Some of us have had an intimate experience with the "dark side" of the church. I wish it were better. I wish it were different. The church can be and often is a wonderfully healthy place to be and to grow. It doesn't pretend to be perfect this side of heaven; if it did, that would be an act of futility. To be honest, I think the rumor that it is or should be perfect is perpetuated by hurts left unhealed and a world in desperate need of reconciliation. Some days, though, even if we absolutely love our churches, we may find ourselves asking the difficult question, "Is church worth all the trouble?"

**EPHESIANS 5:26–27**
"That He might sanctify her, having cleansed her by the washing of water with the word, so that He might present the church to Himself in splendor, without spot or wrinkle or any such thing, that she might be holy and without blemish."

What do you love about your church?

What makes your church difficult at times?

If you are not connected to a church, what keeps you disconnected?

A group of sinners coming together is always going to be just that—a group of sinners coming together. However, when a group of sinners comes together with Christ at the center, *that*, God promises, can be an altogether different—and beautiful—thing.

It's important to be honest about the church on earth so that we can lean in when it's difficult and not jump ship. This flaw-filled institution, the church, was created by God Himself, by the power of the Holy Spirit, as the place where His people come together, as His Bride-to-be. One day, His Bride will stand before Him, and we will all see the Bride Triumphant in the fullest sense alongside the Groom—Jesus Christ—perfect, spotless, blemish free.

Song of Songs 4:1–7 gives us God's perspective of how He sees His Church today. Remember that God had His plan of salvation, through the blood of Jesus Christ, from day one of Creation. That means that God's salvation plan stands strong through the book of Song of Songs and the testimony of the two Lovers. As believers in Christ, we live a now-and-not-yet way of life. We are members of the visible church on earth, which will be imperfect until the Last Day. But God's perspective also sees the invisible Church, which is made up of all *true* believers throughout the earth. Only God can see who truly believes. He calls this Church "altogether beautiful." It is complete, no flaws, because when God looks at us, He sees Jesus' righteousness, not our disunity, caddishness, or differences of opinions.

Glance back at Song of Songs 4:1–7 again. This time, we open the Scripture passage to see the typological metaphor of Christ as the Groom, standing before His Bride, the Church, extolling her beauty.

As you read Song of Songs 4:1–7, write down any theological imagery or any imagery that sounds remotely connected to the Savior.

While we aren't talking definite theological connections here, it is fun to see the way God weaves the Word in surprising ways. Here are a few theological connections I might pull out as I read. In the chart below, read the Song of Songs passage listed and write the possible New Testament connection with the verse given.

| SONG OF SONGS | NEW TESTAMENT CONNECTION |
| --- | --- |
| Song of Songs 4:1—Eyes are doves | Luke 3:22 |
| Song of Songs 4:2—Shorn ewes, come up from the washing | Matthew 9:36 |
| Song of Songs 4:4—Rows of stone | 1 Peter 2:5 |

Now let's look at Ephesians 5 to see more directly what God sees when He looks at His Church. Please read Ephesians 5:25–30. Write out Ephesians 5:29 below.

We have established that many of us have body image issues. Guess what? We also have a *Body of Christ* image issue. It's time to be candid about Ephesians 5:29. How we feel about our own body just might be affecting our lens concerning the Body of Christ. We do not see the Church as God sees her. We see her through our faulty lenses that desire a cultural definition of perfection rather than God's definition.

God cherishes each of us. As we have learned, He calls each of us beautiful. When God looks at each of us, He looks with Christ-shaped lenses. He can only see us as believers through Christ, who is flawless. This is called *attribution*: Christ's quality of perfection, attributed to us. God also *attributes* Christ's flawlessness to the Body of Christ, the Church.

When we look in the mirror of the Law at the church, it looks misshapen, haphazard, struggling at best. When we look in the mirror of the Gospel of Christ at the Church, we see past all the junk.

Use the Bible verses listed to fill in the blanks below to see what God sees when He looks at the Church on earth through the lens of Christ Jesus.

Colossians 3:12
In Christ, the Church is and can be _____
to a hurting world.

1 Timothy 1:15–16
In Christ, the Church is and can give _____
where the world so often lacks it.

2 Corinthians 5:18
In Christ, the Church is and can offer _____
inside and outside her four walls.

**2 CORINTHIANS 13:11**
"Finally, brothers, rejoice. Aim for restoration, comfort one another, agree with one another, live in peace; and the God of love and peace will be with you."

2 Corinthians 13:11
In Christ, the Church is and can be not just a place of _____,
but *the* place of _____ for broken families, broken
hearts, and broken lives.

Christ sacrificed Himself for all of the Church. He sacrificed Himself for you and for me. He sees us as a unified Bride. This is the way He designed life for believers. We are meant to be part of this Church. As much as we or anyone else may try to separate us from the Church on earth by walking away, doing so is only to our deficit. We walk away from the support that God has given us, away from the way God has designed His kingdom work to be carried out. The Church is beautiful to Him, even when I have a hard time seeing it. It is His plan for the continuation of His work on earth. He sees the whole picture. He sees the timeline of here to eternity.

Romans 12 is a Scripture passage about the work and identity of the Church, this beautiful Bride of Christ. Read Romans 12:9–12. How can these short exhortations encourage us to continue to build up the Church today? What exhortation sticks out to you? How could you be a part of bringing that encouragement to your local congregation?

Lastly, return to Song of Songs 4:6. What mountain and hill will the King "go away to," according to this verse?

It was the reformer Martin Luther who held the opinion that myrrh, scripturally, was a symbol for the Word of God, and frankincense was a symbol for prayer. He teaches that these two things bind and unify the Church as she waits for Christ to return for the wedding feast of the Lamb.[30] Remembering our baptismal identity, participating in the Lord's Supper, reading the Word, and coming to God in prayer give us visible, daily assurance that Christ is always at work in His people. He gives love where love is lacking, trust when trust is needed, and unity in seemingly impossible situations.

His work in us, as a Body, as the Bride of Christ, is altogether beautiful.

## Inscribed upon My Heart

Use the Scripture memory verse for the week and the prayer prompt to bring your confession, thanksgiving, praise, and requests before the God who calls you beautiful.

### WEEK 4 MEMORY VERSE

"You are altogether beautiful, my love; there is no flaw in you." Song of Songs 4:7

### PRAYER PROMPT

God, You see a Church without blemish or spot, redeemed fully in Christ Jesus, our Lord . . .

# Day 3

## CAPTIVATING BEAUTY
## SONG OF SONGS 4:8–9

Sometimes the Bible uses language that is hard for us to understand in its fullest sense. We are trapped in reading Scripture with the understanding of our own culture and time. Even with more than a basic understanding of Hebrew and Greek, the languages in which the Bible was originally written, we can easily miss a nuance or context clue. The Bible is a treasure trove of knowledge and intellectual stimulation. And every time you read it, you will discover something new, for God intends for us to discover more and more in our journey through His Word. So, with His Spirit working, we flip open the pages and our minds are ignited with sparks of interest. The Bible itself can be captivating or frustrating or both, all in the same sitting.

That said, I remember being in Sunday School as an adolescent, thinking, "Oh, not this same story again. We do the resurrection every year!" I know, I know . . . not my best moment. Even with God's Spirit living and breathing inside of us, the Old Adam creeps up and we find boredom and disillusionment where there should be none. How do we deal with this?

I think that Song of Songs 4:8–9 can give us some insight. As you read these two verses, write down any invitation Solomon extends.

**AUTHOR'S NOTE**
Words like *justification* and *sanctification* and phrases like *old Adam* can trip us up as we try to study and understand Scripture, leaving us feeling more perplexed than when we started. It's good to dig and search. You can find a helpful terminology list near the front of this study! If you find yourself confused, ask a pastor or someone in your study group; that's why God gave us one another.

Like Solomon's invitation to his bride, faith always starts with God's invitation to us. In Matthew 10, Jesus sent out His first twelve disciples. He told them to go into villages and towns. They were to heal the sick, raise the dead, cleanse lepers, cast out demons, sit with people, build relationships, eat with people, and share the Word with them.

What instructions did He give them in Matthew 10:14?

God gives people the opportunity to reject Him. He invites rather than forces. God *can* work any way He wants. He can rain down fire on Sodom and He can demolish fortresses with a trumpet blast, but this isn't the way He has chosen to reach us. He gives us the gift of His Spirit in our heart, but He won't shove His bread down our throat. Most often, He waits for us to walk deeper into the relationship, even as His Spirit does His work in us. He's patient. He won't take advantage of us the way people do. He honors us by offering affection that is not forced on us.

Were you baptized when you were young? If so, the Spirit has been alive and well in your heart for years. Can you wrap your mind around the grace of that? God brought you to Him before you could even accept the invitation. Maybe you were baptized as an adult, or you are still contemplating Baptism even now. Can you see how God was working on your heart well before you acknowledged it?

While we are still turned away from God, He gently works on us, provides for us, and sustains us through the storms and struggles of life—even if we don't know it. He sends us people to encourage us and to tend to us. He captivates, not because He's pushy, but because He's holy. As Solomon says in Song of Songs 4:8, your heavenly Father waits and calls for you:

## "Come with Me."

Can you remember a time in your life when God invited you through His Word or His people? Please share! Whom has He used to speak the invitation of His grace and love into your life?

I have more good news! He calls to us believers every day, "Come with Me." He invites us to meet with Him and talk with Him, to discover more and more about Him. We grow in the knowledge of His salvation through reading the Bible daily and having daily prayer time, as well as gathering together and meeting with His people around the Word. This is not a far-off idea—to meet with Him regularly. You are doing it right now! And meeting with Him can encompass all of our moments in everyday life.

Read Deuteronomy 6:6–9. What are some of the opportunities you have to live life in daily fellowship with the one whom your soul loves, Christ Jesus?

Which one of these opportunities listed in Deuteronomy have you gravitated to the most in your daily walk of faith?

What new opportunity is offered in Deuteronomy to "Come with Me"—to learn and grow in our God?

Look back at Song of Songs 4:8. According to this verse, from where does God bring us? Fill in the blanks below.

The peak of _____

The peak of _____ and _____

From the _____ of _____

From the _____ of _____

Wondering where these places and peaks are located? See the map in the front of your workbook on page 7.

In 1 Peter 5:8, we find a good cross-reference to the den of lions or mountains of leopards. Whom does Peter warn us about in 1 Peter 5:8?

God brings us from those dangerous places where the devil lurks and attempts to separate us from God. He hides us in the cleft of the rock that is His Word. He is our refuge. He captivates us with security in the knowledge of His forgiveness, of eternity won for us, despite the devil's attempts for our souls. The Lord is steady. Our relationship with Him is ever secure because His offer in Song of Songs 4:8 is constant:

## "Come with Me."

In Christ, the invitation is always there, never to be pulled away from us.

Song of Songs 4:9 gives us further assurance that we are not subject to the grip of the enemy.

Underline or highlight the verb that appears twice in Song of Songs 4:9:

"You have captivated my heart, my sister, my bride; you have captivated my heart with one glance of your eyes, with one jewel of your necklace."

God is captivated with us. Just as Solomon was completely ravished by his bride in these verses, so is our God with His people. He loves you. That's all there is to it. This is made very clear in Romans 8:38–39. Soak it in.

Read Romans 8:38–39. List out what cannot get in the way of God's love for us.

You should have ten things listed. How great is our God's love for us! Can you add anything personal to the list?

What has Satan used in an attempt to separate you from God's love? Maybe it's a person, a temptation, a struggle, anything.

Satan can attempt to place a chasm between you and God's love, but the Truth with a capital *T* is this: nothing can separate you from God's love. While the enemy makes us *feel* like God is absent or unconcerned for us, the Bible assures us that absolutely nothing can separate us from the love of our Savior. God is captivated by you. He doesn't need you, but He wants you. It's a reciprocal relationship that keeps us coming back for more. God's love cannot be ignored. Those early years of opening God's Word to the same story year after year in Sunday School, in Bible study, or all on our lonesome build a foundation to hear Him and grow in Him. God is captivating! We can never have enough. We will never be fully satisfied until we stand in His complete presence on the Last Day.

He is truly captivating and altogether beautiful.

## Inscribed upon My Heart

How are you doing with the Scripture memory verse for the week? Use the verse for the week and the prayer prompt to bring your confession, thanksgiving, praise, and requests before the God who calls you beautiful.

### WEEK 4 MEMORY VERSE

"You are altogether beautiful, my love; there is no flaw in you." Song of Songs 4:7

### PRAYER PROMPT

Lord, we thank You for the place to come and learn and grow and ingest Your Word . . .

# Day 4

## BEAUTY BEYOND WORDS
### SONG OF SONGS 4:9–11

First, you need to know that I love words. I love them, love them, love them, like Eloise loves Nanny, ice cream, and the Plaza Hotel; like hobbits love second breakfast; like Elizabeth Bennett loves books. God could have given us any way to communicate with one another, but He primarily gave us words, and for that, I will be eternally grateful.

The Bible as a book is so interesting. Sometimes it perplexes. Sometimes it astonishes. But no matter its complexity or perplexity, the Word of the Lord always fills and always gives life through its message. Every once in a while, something in it will strike me as just too awe-inspiring to ignore.

When I read Song of Songs 4:9, I couldn't ignore one fun notation in several commentaries. I kept returning to it. It struck me as not only interesting but also meaningful. Let's see what you think about it.

Please write Song of Songs 4:9 in the space below.

לְבַב

*labab*—captivate, unheart, enclose

Circle the word *captivated* in the verse you wrote out above. The Hebrew word for *captivated* in the ESV is *libbabtini*. This word is found only in this verse of Scripture. While that might be ho-hum interesting for you, take note that Matthew Henry describes this word as made-up or created for the expression of this passage.[31]

How fun is that?! A heart too full of love expresses something with a made-up word; words already created weren't enough. Solomon loved his bride; of this we have no doubt. It does not get much more romantic than tongue-tied, unabashed, making-stuff-up love.

The most common translations of the Hebrew word range from "captivated" or "ravished," which most of you see in your Bibles, to "stolen" or "captured." Some translations use words like "charmed" or "taken ahold of." Here's a romantic and fun one from the NASB—"You have made my heart beat faster."

Matthew Henry translates this verse using the words "hearted" and "unhearted" for each use of the Hebrew *libbabtini*, reading something like the following:

> ## "You have hearted my heart, my sister, my bride. You have unhearted my heart with one glance of your eyes." (Heidi's paraphrase)

Doesn't even my translation above seem lacking, insufficient? The love Solomon has for his bride—the love Jesus Christ has for you—is a love that simply defies words. How do we begin to understand this captivating love that God, through Solomon, expresses in this passage? Many commentators reference the connection of love to both the heart and the mind. Love can come through the heart and overflow with emotion, but love can also be a mental exercise, a logical conclusion, whether we feel it or not. In this way, love is seated in the heart and in the mind.[32]

To understand this better, read the passages below from the Song of Songs. Check "Logical" or "Emotional" after each passage, and explain why you chose each label.

Song of Songs 2:4
"He brought me to the banqueting house, and his banner over me was love."
☐ Logical        ☐ Emotional

Song of Songs 5:8
"I adjure you, O daughters of Jerusalem, if you find my beloved, that you tell him I am sick with love."
☐ Logical        ☐ Emotional

Song of Songs 8:6–7
"Set me as a seal upon your heart, as a seal upon your arm, for love is strong as death, jealousy is fierce as the grave. Its flashes are flashes of fire, the very flame of the LORD. Many waters cannot quench love, neither can floods drown it. If a man offered for love all the wealth of his house, he would be utterly despised."
☐ Logical        ☐ Emotional

What did you come up with? The distinction isn't crystal clear, is it? There are times in which we can and should distinguish emotion and reason. When we're feeling overwhelmed by work or household tasks, or when our emotions well up and cause us to lash out at our family or friends, it's helpful to engage our reason. When our friends tell us about struggles they are facing and we want to fix the situations, it is helpful to include our empathetic emotional side in the care we offer them, rather than facts and ideas. It is also useful for us to understand that both logic and emotion go into love. As humans, both are important, and both will fail us.

When have your emotions fooled you into making an unwise decision or speaking rashly to someone you love?

When has your reason led you down the wrong path to overthink, misunderstand, or speak too quickly?

Emotions are a wonderful gift from God. We come to know Him and experience the fullness of life through joy, sorrow, grief, and excitement. Sadness is just as much a gift from Him as happiness because through those emotions, we experience the depth of life. What would life be like without the plethora of emotion that goes into any given day? While it may sound tempting to go a day without so much emotion in it, be it yours or other people's, let's think concretely about it for a moment.

Imagine: What would an emotionless day look like?

It would be like painting a picture all in white paint, with no color to express what the object or the portrait looks like, or gazing at the sunset only to find an all-black sky. It wouldn't be good. We may need less emotion at times. We do not want our emotions to rule us, but we were created *with* them, not sentenced to them like a curse. He knit us in the womb to have the abilities to express love and anger, to weep and to laugh.

Read the following passages. Note what emotive action is involved or what instructions God gives for specific emotions in the passage.

Ecclesiastes 3:4–6




Ephesians 4:26




2 Timothy 1:7

John 11:35




God created emotions, but just like anything else, they shouldn't be our god. We will experience emotional mountaintops as well as deserts in our faith walk. If we trust in our emotions to guide us in this walk, we will never be satisfied. God alone is captivating. He is *labbabtini*. We stand on the firm foundation of Christ Jesus when emotions throw us into turbulence and uncertainty. We rest in His Word and faithfulness in the joys of life as well as the sorrows and all the regular days in between.

Martin Luther, the pastor at the heart of the Reformation in the 1500s, points out in his Small Catechism that our reason and logic also have their place *and* their limits. Glance at page 115 of this workbook to find the Apostles' Creed. Luther's explanation of the Third Article of the Apostles' Creed regarding the Holy Spirit states:

> I believe that I cannot by my own reason or strength believe in Jesus Christ, my Lord, or come to Him; but the Holy Spirit has called me by the Gospel, enlightened me with His gifts, sanctified and kept me in the true faith.[33]

Luther's explanation proclaims the biblical truth that we cannot come to Jesus on our own, no matter how much we know or learn. Just as our heart is not capable of leading us down the right path every time, neither is our brain or mental capabilities. Reason is good, but it is also incomplete.

As much as we'd like to think ourselves wise and we take comfort in knowing God through His Word, only the Spirit creates saving faith.

Compare 1 Corinthians 1:20–25 with Ephesians 2:8–9. Below, write the phrases in each of these passages that teach where salvation comes from and where salvation does not come from.

Salvation comes from . . .

Salvation does not come from . . .

And so we are not ruled by our hearts *or* our minds. We are ruled by Christ. At the end of the day, when we mess up, when we think the wrong thing or misplace our trust or let our emotions wreak havoc—we stand on Christ. We are captivated by His Spirit and we joyfully can only say, "Thank You."

Jesus invites us in the words of His Father:

## "Love the Lord your God with all your heart and with all your soul and with all your mind and with all your strength." Mark 12:30

Only through Him can we even begin to love. Through Him, we are captivated by the Spirit's work. He gave Himself to be sacrificed on the cross because He treasures all of you—your heart, soul, mind, and your strength.

Song of Songs 4:9 points us to a God who was so captivated with His creation that He gave His only Son, Christ Jesus, so that His Church, His people, can be captivated by Him as our Savior.

God cannot be left speechless. He can create whatever words He wants to express His love for His people. His wisdom and heart are well beyond ours. Inexpressible. Indescribable. That is our God. We are the ones left speechless, captivated by Him, which is altogether beautiful.

## Inscribed upon My Heart

Use the Scripture memory verse for the week and the prayer prompt to bring your confession, thanksgiving, praise, and requests before the God who calls you beautiful.

### WEEK 4 MEMORY VERSE

"You are altogether beautiful, my love; there is no flaw in you." Song of Songs 4:7

### PRAYER PROMPT

Lord, I reflect on Your words today, especially . . .

# Day 5

## BEAUTIFUL ENDEARMENTS
## SONG OF SONGS 4:10–16

Song of Songs is a book full of metaphors and endearments. Perhaps you have been shaking your fists at this book, wondering when I was going to start explaining what "hair like a flock of goats" means for your life today or what the "peaks of Amana and Senir" have to do with the Church.

I haven't done this for one main reason: there is a limit to metaphor, and we dare not take each word too literally in and of itself. Remember, the book is poetic. It is best taken as a beautifully expressive whole, while appreciating the nuances of each chapter and verse.

That said, there are metaphors in the Bible that are repeated often, and so we will dive deeper into those. The Scriptures offer expanded understanding regarding these particular metaphors, and cross-references can offer solid definitions. These metaphors are also often attached to the other language tool we see in the Song of Songs—endearments. An endearment is any term or title of affection.

Modern endearments include names such as *dear*, *darling*, and *honey*. What endearments does your husband, parent, or another loved one use for you? What endearments do you use for others?

Endearments are intended to make us feel special and connected. Endearments are almost always an expression of relationship; otherwise, they can be offensive, such as the stranger who calls you "honey" in the grocery store. That's just annoying at the very least.

Read Song of Songs 4:10–16, and list the terms of endearment you find in the passage. Consider this activity a scavenger hunt of the ancient text. What special names does Solomon call his love in the reading?

Let's broaden the scavenger hunt. Skim through the Song of Songs as a whole. What endearments can you find? I listed a few verses below to get you started. Feel free to do a seek-and-find throughout the book if you would like.

Song of Songs 1:7–8

Song of Songs 2:10

Song of Songs 5:2

Song of Songs 7:1

Endearments are a way for Solomon and his bride to express things that are difficult to put into words. No one word, no expression of relationship, is complete enough to describe the love Solomon has for his bride. Instead, he gives numerous endearments to express the multidimensional quality of his relationship with the Shulammite.

God the Father has the same reaction toward His people. God the Son, Christ Jesus, has the same love for His Church. We know this not only because of our interpretation of the Song of Songs but also because of the metaphors and endearments throughout Scripture.

Let's take time to study three biblical metaphors that are also endearments.

## GOD IS OUR SHEPHERD, AND WE ARE HIS SHEEP.

As sheep, we are slightly ignorant, continuously wandering, and often in needing of being rescued from trouble. *Sheep* does not seem to be the most flattering of endearments. However, it does describe a special and caring relationship we have with our Lord!

Read the following Scriptures, and note the benefits of being God's sheep in each one.

Psalm 95:6–7

Matthew 18:12–14

Luke 12:32

## WE ARE GOD'S TREASURE.

The gift of salvation is given to us through Christ's redemptive work on the cross. Redemption, by definition, is paying for something that is valuable. Christ Jesus has paid for us by His death and fought our battles for us in this life, all while we remain completely unworthy. Yet, He deems us worthwhile, a precious treasure. Let's look at an instance of Scripture interpreting Scripture.

Look up the following two passages, and write the words or phrases that are repeated in each.

Deuteronomy 7:6

1 Peter 2:9–10

Thank goodness for the Bible. In the fullness of time, God brings forth His plan and the full understanding of His work to His people. When He comes back for us on the Last Day, we will see it all laid out before us. It will all be crystal clear. Until then, God gives us His Word to help us understand His relationship with us.

## WE (THE CHURCH) ARE THE BRIDE OF CHRIST.

Read Ephesians 5:22–33. We have studied this passage plenty already because the marriage relationship is central to the Song of Songs, but let's look with fresh eyes. As you read the passage, identify how the Church's relationship with Christ is like marriage.

List below each descriptor you come across in Ephesians 5:22–33.

Now, fill in the missing words from Ephesians 5:32 below.

"This _____  _____

_____, and I am saying that it refers to Christ and the

church."

Christ, the Church, marriage, and the comingling of these is a mystery.

We are not going to completely understand how it works. This is something studying the Song of Songs teaches us. We don't have to understand the meaning for every reference to a flock of goats or a gazelle leaping or a mountain peak. Does each of these share with us something about Christ? Yes, because all of Scripture points to Christ, but commentators argue different interpretations of each one. Sometimes Scripture is about as clear as mud. Beautifully, God invites us to live in the mystery with Christ at the center.

As Solomon calls his love both his sister and his bride, two seemingly incongruent relationships, so is God's relationship with us. We, as the Church, are His Bride. We are also His children. We are His people. We are His treasured possession. We are His sheep.

He is our rock. He is our fortress. He is *our* treasure. He is our potter. The Bible uses metaphor to give us snippets of a relationship so unexplainable, so altogether beautiful, that no one term can describe it.

## Inscribed upon My Heart

Use the Scripture memory verse for the week and the prayer prompt to bring your confession, thanksgiving, praise, and requests before the God who calls you beautiful.

### WEEK 4 MEMORY VERSE

"You are altogether beautiful, my love; there is no flaw in you." Song of Songs 4:7

### PRAYER PROMPT

Lord, I am Your sheep, Your treasured possession, Your child . . .

you are altogether beautiful, my love; there is no flaw in you.

# Week 5
## GOD OVER ALL

# Viewer Guide

## VIDEO 5: FOLLY AND FORGIVENESS
## SONG OF SONGS 5:1–8

**Verses to Bookmark**
Song of Songs 4:16; 5:1–8
Romans 7:15–20
2 Corinthians 5:17–19
Romans 8:26–27

Song of Songs 5:1 is an _____.

Invitation is important in any stage of _____. The ongoing reciprocity of _____ and _____ in a relationship is vital.

**Old Adam & New Adam**
Check out the Useful Terms on pages 8–9 for a refresher on the old Adam and new Adam.

## THE OLD ADAM AND THE NEW ADAM

WE LIVE IN THE REALITY OF THE OLD ADAM.

Our foolishness just is. We are foolish by _____.

The old Adam makes _____.

We can't get out of bed on _____ _____. If it were up to us to save ourselves, we'd be a disaster.

On our own, we aren't able to respond to God. Only by the power of the Holy Spirit working in us can we respond and grow in our relationship with Him. But take heart! He is at work in you!

We are often _____ and _____.

At the heart of this struggle is that the Shulammite woman does not understand the _____ of her beloved.

Her lover doesn't need pretty scents. He simply wants her. In the same way, God does not need us to be ready.

WE LIVE IN THE FORGIVENESS OF THE NEW ADAM.

We are _____ in Christ.

Our foolishness is seen now through Christ's unwavering strength and wisdom.

We are old Adam and new Adam, _____ and _____.

## DISCUSSION QUESTIONS

1. When have we responded like the Shulammite to those who matter most in our lives? We often put things, entertainment, and work before people, who matter so much more. What kind of impact does this have on our relationships?

2. When do we respond to God like this? When do we say thank You, but no thank You to the lover of our souls? What have we put before Him?

3. Where have you seen God work His forgiveness despite your foolishness?

# Day 1

## OUR CALM PLACE
### SONG OF SONGS 5:1

I have a calm place. It features a nature trail, a beautiful sunrise, crunchy leaves, and a fresh fall breeze. Colors of red, orange, and yellow surround me. Can you hear the crunch of leaves on the path? I can.

I have a friend who goes to the beach in her head. She imagines the roar of the waves and the sand between her toes. She can feel the sun on her face, and just imagining this wonderful scene helps her take a deep breath and step back from the stress in front of her.

Do you have a calm place in your mind, a mental image that relaxes you in the middle of life's stresses? You may not call it your "calm place," but I'm talking about a place you can go in your mind when life gets stressful and you just need a moment. It's really a daydream, a good use of your imagination, but it is just that—useful. Your calm place may have sounds, textures, sights, or even smells that help you to relax and recover your wits after—or in the middle of—a stressful situation.

Whether or not you've thought of one before, describe your "calm place."

When I imagine my calm place, I hear Jesus' words in Matthew 11:28–30:

"Come to Me, all who labor and are heavy laden, and I will give you rest. Take My yoke upon you, and learn from Me, for I am gentle and lowly in heart, and you will find rest for your souls. For My yoke is easy, and My burden is light."

Jesus invites us to find a place of rest in Him, in the midst of all of life's chaos. He won't take us out of this world until it's time (John 17:15), but we have a safe place, a place of calm and warmth, to rest with Him in His Word while we complete His kingdom work here on this planet, in this life we've been given.

The Lovers in the Song of Songs have their own calm place, whether it's literal—a place they go together—or figurative, like the ones in our heads.

Read Song of Songs 5:1. What visual images or activities are identified in this verse?

The Lovers have a calm place apart from the world. They come together in this place that is filled with love to rejoice in each other. They drink of affection and contentment in the safety of each other. The garden in the Song of Songs is always a vision of lushness, a place where things grow and thrive. Song of Songs 5:1 pushes the play button, if you will, on our senses of sight, sound, taste, smell, and touch. Can you smell the myrrh in the verse? Can you feel the sticky honey dripping from the honeycomb? Can you taste the wine? see the creamy milk? By the time you get to the concluding sentence in the verse, you almost feel like you could cup your hands and drink love up!

The vivid language of this chorus places us in the context of the Scripture *with* the Lovers.

Do you have places or people that make you feel loved, safe, thriving? Think of those with whom you like to gather. Who offers you a nonjudgmental space, lets you be yourself, or shares with you truth in love?

God gives each of us people in our lives who offer us this garden of safety. Maybe you have just one of these people in your life; maybe you have several. No matter how many or how few, you can rest in the knowledge that you have a relationship that offers more safety than any human relationship on this earth ever could. Having a relationship with Christ Jesus opens the door to freedom and life, real living, in a way we won't understand in its fullest sense until we get to heaven, but we sure don't want to miss out on that relationship now. When you come to Him with your confession, seeking relationship, He is always safe, warm, and inviting.

Look up the following Scripture passages, and share what you find in each verse regarding affection, care, and safety within your relationship with God and your relationships with people.

| OUR RELATIONSHIP WITH GOD |
| --- |
| John 15:12–15, 26–27 |
| Ruth 1:6–18 |
| Romans 12:9–13 |
| OUR RELATIONSHIPS WITH PEOPLE |
| John 15:12–15, 26–27 |
| Ruth 1:6–18 |
| Romans 12:9–13 |

We were created by God for His glory alone, but He designed us to be in relationship with people in order to share His love and discover more about Him as we study His Word together and support and encourage one another. For a moment, let's focus on our horizontal, earthly relationships.

In the following space, work through three of your relationships, and consider individually how each of these relationships can be built up. How can each relationship be a place where God encourages and gives peace, where we can offer and be offered His tender loving care through one another? The relationship may be a spouse, a friend, a parent, a sibling, a mentor, anyone. I'll give you an example to get you started:

Relationship: *My friend Sarah*
Location: *She's in Texas. I live in Nebraska.*

What I can share with Sarah in safety and the full knowledge that I am loved:
*Struggles with my marriage and parenting*
*Body image issues*
*Writing and professional ideas*

How do we build each other up and encourage each other?

*Text daily for encouragement and check in*

*Pray for each other's spouses and professional dreams*

*Goal to visit once a year face-to-face*

How could we encourage each other more?

*Text one another prayers, or call and pray together*

*Send a Bible verse of the day for each other*

*Be more available for phone calls*

Your turn! Choose the relationships you'd like to focus on and answer the questions for each.

Relationship:

Location:

What I can share with this person in safety and the full knowledge that I am loved:

How do we build each other up and encourage each other?

How could we encourage each other more?

Relationship:

Location:

What I can share with this person in safety and the full knowledge that I am loved:

How do we build each other up and encourage each other?

How could we encourage each other more?

Relationship:

Location:

What I can share with this person in safety and the full knowledge that I am loved:

How do we build each other up and encourage each other?

There are only so many of these precious people in our lives. Thank you for sharing some of yours. Each of those relationships is a gift from God. He works through the lives of all of those around us, whether they know it or not!

Remember, even when we feel like relationships are a struggle and we are alone in this world, Jesus beckons us to come to Him, to rest in His garden of grace. Come to the garden of His Word! Drink and eat at His table in Holy Communion. Be wrapped in His affection through absolution, the forgiveness of your sins.

The joy of meeting with Him in the garden alone or through the gift of the Body of Christ is altogether beautiful.

## INSCRIBED UPON MY HEART

Use the Scripture memory verse for the week and the prayer prompt to bring your confession, thanksgiving, praise, and requests before the God who calls you beautiful.

### WEEK 5 MEMORY VERSE

"What is your beloved more than another beloved, O most beautiful among women? What is your beloved more than another beloved, that you thus adjure us?" Song of Songs 5:9

### PRAYER PROMPT

Lord in heaven, thank You for all of the people You have put into my life. I especially thank You for . . .

**ABOUT THIS VERSE**
God is not one god in a pantheon of gods or the buffet of gods we find in the world. He is Yahweh, the God of the universe, one God in Trinity—Father, Son, and Holy Spirit. He is so much more than anything else this life could offer us.

# Day 2

## OUR WATCHMAN
## SONG OF SONGS 5:2–8

No one likes a bully. That's just the way the watchmen in Song of Songs 5:7 seemed to me the first time I read the chapter—great big ol' bullies.

Read Song of Songs 5:2–8. What sticks out to you about the watchmen?

Today we will focus on those watchmen to sort through another vantage point of Song of Songs 5. In my opinion, Song of Songs 5:2–8 is one of the hardest passages to read in the Song because the violence seems nonsensical. The woman hears her Beloved knock at the door; she wants to get up but foolishly is concerned about her fresh garment. By the time she gets to the door, her Lover is gone. She's disappointed and runs after him. At first glance, verse 7 seems oddly out of place.

List below the three things the watchmen do to the Shulammite in Song of Songs 5:7.

The actions taken against the woman in this verse are abhorrent to most of us when we read it—vulgar beatings, bruises, ripping off a veil. Who steals a woman's veil? Goodness me. To understand this passage and some possible significance in the context of the Church and our lives today, we need to analyze the role of these watchmen as well as some uncomfortable stuff, such as our understanding of protection and violence.

## Watchmen in the Old Testament

I'm not sure we can fully appreciate the necessity of watchmen with our twenty-first-century perspective. Perhaps soldiers and those who have lived through active wartime have a better understanding. Take a moment to understand the watchmen's context.

Look at the following verses for some insight. What was the watchman's duty in each passage?

2 Kings 9:17–20

1 Samuel 14:2, 15–17

Using the insight of these verses, describe in your own words the watchmen of the Old Testament and their role.

הַשֹּׁמְרִים
*hashomerim*: to keep, watch, preserve[34]

In the Old Testament times, battle was constant. Cities were continuously on guard, waiting for attack. Kingdoms wanted to dominate neighboring kingdoms—for trade, for resources, for slaves, and for better geographic situations to prevent other attacks. Safety and peace were realities under some kings, including Solomon, but even during times of peace, watchmen had the duty to persevere through the day and through the night, always watching for danger, for enemies, and for visitors of any kind.[35] Safety was a reality because of people like the watchmen.

At the end of verse 7, we find a clue that these particular watchmen were "watchmen of the walls." Because we think it is likely that the Song is about King Solomon, it is also likely that the walls are the walls of Jerusalem, which was the hub of the nation of Israel throughout the kingdoms of David and Solomon. These watchmen had to keep this very large city safe. They were witnesses to the actions that took place in the dark of night, and they guarded the people in more ways than one: they kept the city safe from those outside the walls and from those within the walls. This leads us to two theories about the watchmen in the Song of Songs and why they did what they did to the Shulammite.

These watchmen answered to the king. They had the duty not only to keep Jerusalem safe but also to keep the individuals who resided inside the walls safe from would-be troublemakers. The female Beloved in the Song of Songs, in her passionate pursuit of her husband, did not think before running out into the night. Her nighttime quest could easily have been misunderstood by onlookers as the king's wife gone out for a questionable liaison. Or imagine the trouble that would have occurred if the king's wife became vulnerable to attackers and enemies at the gate. By running out into the night, she put herself and all those within the city in danger. These watchmen were like the Secret Service for their king and queen. If something happened to her, the entire nation of Israel would have been affected.

Putting this into our context today, imagine if we had no concern for what happened in the lives of those around us. Without pointing fingers and publicly declaring someone's struggle, what if we never addressed anyone's sin, including our own? It may help to make the connection by looking again at Song of Songs 5:6–7.

Just like the Shulammite, every single one of us has at some point run not to God in our foolishness, but out into the night, searching after other things to solve our problems and heal our pain.

How often do you run foolishly to other things, people, or places instead of to the arms of your Savior? Where, what, or whom do you run to when you are in pain or need help, rather than running to God and asking Him for help?

The Shulammite may seem to be an innocent victim in Song of Songs 5, but she also may have been thinking only of her own needs when she should have been thinking of the other residents of the city. Because of her rash actions, the entire city might have experienced the consequences of the Shulammite acting without really thinking. The watchmen, while overzealous, may have been, in the Old Testament context, just doing their job. Most of us have a strong distaste for violence, and rightly so, but it's helpful to understand that cultures and contexts, historically and currently, may operate differently than our own.

THEORY NO. 2: THEY ARE WATCHMEN WITH EVIL INTENT.

Enter violence, stage left.

It's uncomfortable, isn't it?

The watchmen beat her and stole her veil. Commentators encourage us to look further beyond an individual understanding of the story here. This may be a metaphoric image of persecution in the Church. Just as we think, "Who in the world would have evil intent for this poor woman, searching for her Lover?" we wonder, "Who in the world would have evil intent against the Church?"

What kind of arguments or acts of violence in our modern day have you heard about against the Church itself or those associated with the Church as believers in Jesus Christ? How would you respond if put in a position of individual persecution?

Persecution of the Church is real, both from outside and from within the Church. People die daily for their faith in many countries, and churches close all too frequently because of a few angry wolves among sheep. No matter the situation though, God's Word goes out, in spite of and because of the struggle of persecution. We pray for it to end. We pray for countries where Bibles are illegal and death is the consequence for faith in Jesus. We pray for those who are mistreated, tortured, sued, publicly humiliated, and oppressed; we pray for those who give their lives for the testimony of Christ.

We pray over our churches and our pastors and leaders. We remember that God is faithful and nothing—absolutely nothing—done in the name of Jesus Christ is done in vain. Read Romans 8:26–28 with fresh eyes.

What if our weaknesses were not just personal, but collective also? How does this verse apply to the Church on earth?

We are weak, like the Shulammite woman and the residents of the city in the Song of Songs. They needed the watchmen to look over them and warn them of danger. We need the Holy Spirit, one another, and the angels unseen around us to alert the King of kings and gather the troops together to fight the good fight against Satan and his army.

Bring it, Satan. We are the Church.

Who is our watchman? Fill in the missing words in Psalm 121:7–8 below using the ESV translation.

"The _____ will _____ you from all evil;

_____ will _____ your life.

The _____will _____

your _____  _____

and your _____  _____

from _____  _____

forth and _____."

 

The Lord keeps. He keeps each of us, and He keeps His Church. He is our watchman. He shows us our sin, speaking the truth in love in His Word. He uses those around us to bring us back when we have run into the night. He is different from the watchmen the Shulammite encountered. He isn't violent or aggressive. He took on all the beatings and all the violence in His death on the cross. He offers us forgiveness and mercy. He watches as we go out and as we come in, from the city gates to the rural farms, from the mountaintop to the bottom of the sea, today and every day to come. Our watchman, the Lord of all the earth, is altogether beautiful.

## Inscribed upon My Heart

Use the Scripture memory verse for the week and the prayer prompt to bring your confession, thanksgiving, praise, and requests before the God who calls you beautiful.

### WEEK 5 MEMORY VERSE

"What is your beloved more than another beloved, O most beautiful among women? What is your beloved more than another beloved, that you thus adjure us?" Song of Songs 5:9

### PRAYER PROMPT

Dear Lord, You are the watchman of my soul. I place my trust in You . . .

# Day 3

OUR "MORE THAN" GOD
**SONG OF SONGS 5:9**

I am a sucker for a good chorus. I like all kinds of music, and one of my favorite things to do is belt out a show tune or familiar song while I drive or clean the house. There is something about the cadence of a chorus. It can be both familiar and comforting, as well as bold and empowering.

When I was a little girl, I remember my dad sitting next to me in church. His strong presence was something I took for granted until I moved away and had to sit in a row all by my lonesome. My dad isn't a vocalist, but my adult ears can still hear him loudly singing the words to a familiar hymn often sung during the Lord's Supper at our church:

## "LORD, MAY THY BODY AND THY BLOOD BE FOR MY SOUL THE HIGHEST GOOD!"[36]

You probably can't hear my dad in your ear right now like I can. Whom in your life can you hear singing out beside you? What other memories does this bring to mind?

Loud and proud. That's how I would describe my dad's baritone. Proud of all the Lord had done for him and oblivious to the off notes or accidental key changes. His song pointed others to the one he was praising.

This is also how I would describe the Others' chorus in Song of Songs 5:9, which is our memory verse for the week. The Others' job is to prop up the insight of the Shulammite bride, to prepare the audience for the song of praise she is about to sing, and to point the audience to the one she is praising. The Others' song in this verse is intended to be hypothetical, not literal. After all, they have seen Solomon ride in for his wedding surrounded by his mighty men. They have seen his strength, his imposing wealth. They know the answer to the questions they ask in the passage below before they ask them.

Fill in the missing pieces of Song of Songs 5:9 in the blanks below.

"What is your_____ _____

_____ _____ _____,

O most beautiful among women?

What is your_____ _____

_____ _____ _____,

that you thus adjure us?"

## "More than another beloved." Song of Songs 5:9

Normally, I avoid the comparison game. Nothing good can come from it. In our society, we compare homes and decor, educations and jobs, families and children. We submit ourselves to needless anxiety and wantonness as we open the door to the lusty master named Comparison. Comparison is the thief of grace as much as it is the thief of joy. We easily miss opportunities to give others mercy and grace when we are so busy trying to one-up them. Comparison is stealthy and silent. He slips in the door quietly as the judge of others. He speaks pretty words in our head that often prop us up and tear others down.

"I wouldn't let my child act like that."

"I'm glad my hair isn't cut like that!"

"We might not have as much money, but at least we're happier than that couple."

"I wouldn't go to that church, live in that place, shop at that store . . ."

Often, we never notice Comparison's presence until frustration and discontent wash over us. Comparison is such a common problem that it gets two Commandments all to itself—Nine and Ten.

> **COMPARE**
> To define, measure, and estimate a person or thing in relation to another person or thing, finding what is similar and what is different and judging it based on these similarities and differences.

What are we told not to covet in Commandments Nine and Ten? Fill in what you remember. If you'd like a little help, read Exodus 20:17.

Thou shalt not covet . . .

Yep, at the heart of comparison is greed—always wanting more than God intended for us, more than what's best for us, more than what we need. Which item listed in the commandments do you struggle with the most? Circle it above.

## "What is your beloved more than another beloved?" Song of Songs 5:9

The difference between our comparison and the one found in Song of Songs 5:9 is that the Song props up rather than tears down. The Others aren't asking a flippant and prissy question, challenging the Shulammite to prove her Lover's worth. Instead, they are asking so that she has a platform on which to extol him. In offering the question, they also point us directly to the Savior—our "more than" kind of God.

The Shulammite's response to this chorus is straightforward. My paraphrase of Song of Songs 5:10–16 might go something like this: "Well, let me tell you. His complexion, his hair, his eyes, his smile, his kissable lips, he's so muscular, he's so strong—that's my beloved! *Did you not notice? Is it not obvious?* He is utterly magnificent . . . since you asked."

We'll talk more about the details about the Beloved listed in verses 10–16 in tomorrow's study, for the enamored bride puts it so much more beautifully than I. For today, however, let's continue to focus on the Others' chorus in verse 9. In particular, let's look at the application of the Song as a typological metaphor of Christ and His Church and from our place as children praising an awesome God. How would we answer the Others' hypothetical questions?

"What is your beloved more than another beloved?"

"What is this Christ, more than another prophet?"

"Who is this God, more than another god?"

Oh boy! Don't even get me started. I may not be able to stop.

How about you? How does our God compare with all the other options in the buffet of gods and religions that abound in our world?

I just love when people ask me what makes Jesus different from another prophet or another "good man" who walked the earth. It's a wide-open opportunity for Him to shine bright.

One easy way to answer this burning question is with another question:

# "WHAT'S IN A NAME?"

NAMES FOR JESUS
CHRIST
Son of God
Son of Man
Lamb of God
The truth
Bread of life
Redeemer
King of kings
Light of the world
Great High Priest
Messiah

One online Bible dictionary lists more than 900 names for God in the entirety of Scripture.[37] Nine hundred! These aren't separate ideas of who God is or what God does. These are integrated names for the persons of the Trinity and their work from creation to the Last Day and into the new creation—900! Are you just as amazed by this as I am? I may or may not be writing this with my mouth hanging open.

Let's cut this down to something more manageable in one small day's homework. Bibleresources.org gives us a list of about 105 names for Jesus in the Bible,[38] and biblegateway.com[39] lists about 60 names for Jesus, organized by theme, considering both Testaments of Scripture. Today, we'll rest on 3 names that stand out and boldly bring the truth of who God is into our world when we share them.

## THE WORD

This name for Jesus may be one of the most important for our understanding of Scripture and its importance in our daily lives. Jesus as the Word so clearly shows the seamless way in which God connects all the dots in the Bible and in His plan for salvation, as well as in our lives and . . . it's just plain cool. We cannot be confronted with Jesus as the Word and not stand in awe of God, just as the Shulammite stood before her groom. I'll let Scripture lay out the connecting points for you.

Look up the following verses, and write what each verse teaches us about Jesus as the Word, which is also the Bible.

John 1:1–4

Psalm 33:4

Hebrews 4:12

2 Timothy 3:16–17

Jesus was the Word since before the beginning of creation. This is His name. He was there when all the universe was formed, as the Word, when all the plans were laid out. In His incarnation, Jesus became the Word made flesh. He dwelt with us and among us as a child, an adolescent, a grown man. He physically died and physically rose, for the sake of the salvation of all people. When He speaks, He speaks the Word. He also breathes the Word. He embodies the Word. He proclaims the Word. He is the Word. Jesus is in our hearts and souls and minds through the Spirit's indwelling in us, but He is also in our laps as we open the Scriptures. As we read and digest the words of the Bible, He works like the blade of a surgeon, cutting into our lives, healing and molding and making new.

It sounds too simplistic to say that it is all mind-bending. Jesus as the Word is a large concept to take in, but at the same time it's simple—Jesus is the Word made flesh. He is the bread of life, the Word I eat in the Lord's Supper, the breath of life I breathe each day, the Word on my lap. He is my lamp and my guide. He is in everything, and everything ultimately points to Him.

# "WHAT IS YOUR BELOVED MORE THAN ANOTHER BELOVED?"
## MY BELOVED IS EVERYTHING.

### SAVIOR

Let me illustrate the importance of this name with a story. Our local library had an Earth Day celebration. My family and I are fans of stewarding this lovely planet and its resources, so we went. As soon as we walked into the library, the kids eagerly scrambled to the coloring table and picked out a printed sheet to color. My oldest daughter picked up a coloring sheet with "Save the Earth" in big bubble letters across the top. As if in a chorus, all four of my children joined together, "We know, we know, Mom, only Jesus saves." Perhaps I have reiterated this point a teensy bit much in our house, but it's vital that we understand—only Jesus saves, but oh, does He save.

We have one Lord and one Savior. We'll never be good enough or do enough good to save ourselves, much less the earth or anything else. God has called us, gathered us, redeemed us, and set us free from guilt and shame in Christ Jesus. I'll let the Word speak for itself.

Read the following verses, and write what each verse tells us about Jesus as our Savior.

Matthew 1:21

Acts 4:12

Philippians 3:20

God saves us through Jesus, once and for all time, on the cross. He sent Jesus to die and then to rise to give us hope and new life. And He continues to send Jesus' love and affection—through His Word and the people of the Body of Christ—to remind us of who we are as children of the Most High God. Jesus saves. It is who He is and what He does.

## "WHAT IS YOUR BELOVED MORE THAN ANOTHER BELOVED?"
### *MY BELOVED SAVES.*

I Am

The name "I am" is a prophetic fulfillment that binds the Old and New Testaments together seamlessly. It also connects Jesus very clearly to God the Father. This name crosses the breadth of Scripture, from Exodus to the Gospels to Revelation. Even if the following verses are not new to you at all, ask God to give you a little awe at the reminder of the way God weaves His truth so seamlessly through Scripture. It really is remarkable.

First, read Exodus 3:13–14, and answer the following questions.

What did God tell Moses His name was?

To whom did God send Moses to proclaim this name? Why?

Hundreds of years pass by, and God sends His Son, born of a virgin and named Jesus, to be the Savior of the world.

Read the following verses from the Book of John, and underline the names Jesus calls Himself in each one.

John 6:48: "I am the bread of life."

John 8:12: "Again Jesus spoke to them, saying, 'I am the light of the world. Whoever follows Me will not walk in darkness, but will have the light of life.'"

John 10:7: "So Jesus again said to them, 'Truly, truly, I say to you, I am the door of the sheep.'"

John 10:11: "I am the good shepherd. The good shepherd lays down His life for the sheep."

John 11:25: "Jesus said to her, 'I am the resurrection and the life. Whoever believes in Me, though he die, yet shall he live.'"

John 14:6: "Jesus said to him, 'I am the way, and the truth, and the life. No one comes to the Father except through Me.'"

John 15:1: "I am the true vine, and My Father is the vinedresser."

Look up John 8:58. Record the words of Jesus below.

"I am the light, I am the door, I am the good shepherd, I am the way, I am the truth." Our God in Trinity is the complete fulfillment of all the I ams there ever could be. "I am" is not just one name of Jesus. It is every name of Jesus. He is so big, so holy, so wonderful that putting Him into any one name can never be done.

What has Christ done in your life? How has He risen above other beloveds and shown Himself to be true God to you personally? Record a small sampling of His work in you below.

# "I AM has sent me to you."

## "I AM WHO I AM." Exodus 3:14

The fullness of eternity is written across the pages of the Bible you hold in your laps. "What is your beloved more than another beloved?" He is altogether beautiful.

## Inscribed upon My Heart

How are you doing with the Scripture memory verse for the week? Use this verse and the prayer prompt to bring your confession, thanksgiving, praise, and requests before the God who calls you beautiful.

### WEEK 5 MEMORY VERSE

"What is your beloved more than another beloved, O most beautiful among women? What is your beloved more than another beloved, that you thus adjure us?" Song of Songs 5:9

### PRAYER PROMPT

Lord Jesus Christ, the great "I am," You are . . .

# Day 4

## OUR INDIVIDUALITY, OUR RECIPROCITY
## SONG OF SONGS 5:10–16

I remember the day like it was yesterday. I had just put on a new dress. It was strapless and slim, gray with thin white stripes, and ended just below the knees. I zipped it up, spun around once, and immediately felt good about myself. *This dress rocks!* My husband walked into the room shortly after and promptly asked, "Is the front of that dress supposed to do that weird thing?"

*Um, excuse me. I am rocking this dress, sir.*

My husband and I obviously have different tastes. What he finds attractive at times is quite a bit different from what I would find attractive. He likes beards and doesn't understand why I find them itchy and slightly unkempt in almost every case. (I apologize in advance, bearded men everywhere.) Dave thinks decorative pillows should never be a thing. In his mind, pillows are made to sleep on, and "extras" are nuisances that need to be picked up, moved around, and needlessly rearranged. For me, the more pillows the better. They are so pretty and cozy. I bought Dave a pair of deck shoes, thinking they would be casual and classy. Him, not so much. I like lipstick that pops, a fun and perhaps shocking color, but I gave it up for my husband, who likes my lips as natural as possible. So when my husband responded so apathetically to my dress, I could only look at him and wonder how in the world we were so different. In such instances, I simply remind myself that God created us to be complements, not clones. In the end, I spun around in my dress once more, smiled, and said, "I think it fits perfectly."

Solomon and the Shulammite were two different people as well. They don't extol the same qualities in each other. The Shulammite appreciates different things about Solomon than he appreciates about her. In today's reading, we get to hear from her. When the Others ask the Shulammite a very personal question, "What is your beloved more than another beloved?" she responds with a list. Song of Songs 5:10–16 records how she responded to the Others' question—they gave her an opportunity to extol this Beloved of hers, and she goes for it. These verses give us a list of Solomon's physical qualities from her perspective.

Quickly glance through Song of Songs 5:10–16. What qualities does she mention in this passage?

It is interesting to compare the Song of Songs 5 list with the list of the Shulammite's qualities that Solomon extols in Song of Songs 4:1–7. Each list begins with the face and moves downward, getting more personal and intimate as it goes.

Do you spot any similarities if you look at both passages? any glaring differences?

What can we learn from a list? These lists, while metaphorically and poetically beautiful, also teach us in a very practical way about two important qualities in relationships: reciprocity and individuality.

## Reciprocity

In the secular world, if you google *reciprocity*, you'll find definitions about countries making agreements and people making arrangements. You'll also find phrases such as "I'll scratch your back if you scratch mine." In God's economy, as usual, things look a little different.

The Lovers in the Song of Songs may be extolling physical qualities they see and enjoy in their mate, but they do so in order to honor each other. God's reciprocity is always concerned with giving honor—to Him, of course, to His name, yes, but also that we might honor one another as His children. Reciprocity, the back-and-forth of a relationship of any kind, whether our relationship with God or with others, is intended to build up as well as be a source of enjoyment in our lives.

Read about the way God sees honor working in relationships in Romans 12:10. Write that verse below.

*Outdo, not simply make do*. This is God's breed of reciprocity. The problem with "I'll scratch your back if you scratch mine" in relationship is that the lowest expectations win. If one member of the relationship is grumpy, the other eventually settles for grumpy as status quo. If everything revolves around equity, and one constantly tears the other down, eventually, at some point, one quits trying to build the other one up. But imagine reciprocity in a relationship ruled by grace instead of equity. You can envision the Lovers' discourse in the Song of Songs as them trying to one-up each other in compliments—not false compliments, mind you, not flattery, but genuine kindness and honor.

Where else in the Bible do we learn about reciprocity Christ's way? Read the following three passages and note the relationship addressed by each one, as well as any words that stick out to you in each verse.

Titus 2:11–15

2 Corinthians 6:11–13

1 Samuel 14:6–7

All of these passages cover different relationships—with Christ, with other believers in the Body of Christ, and with friends. How does the wisdom of each verse flow over into other relationships though?

What does "hearts wide open" look like in marriage? This is an interesting question to consider whether you are married or not. Please share your thoughts.

What does "hearts wide open" look like in friendship?

How does "I am with you heart and soul" look in the Body of Christ, within your local church specifically?

We have a Lord and Savior who went beyond reciprocity to bring us honor!

## "For the grace of God has appeared, bringing salvation for all people." Titus 2:11

This—grace—is how God deems to bring reciprocity into our relationship with Him; He does not ask us to work hard at becoming worthy. We don't need to pretty ourselves up for God. (You can read more on this on p. 170.) Instead, Jesus sacrificed Himself so that we may have a relationship with God—a relationship where there is an exchange of love and affection, not to mention the back-and-forth of communication through prayer and His Word.

Our relationships with people on this earth will require work. Relationships are experiential, and they look a whole lot better when they are filled with self-sacrifice instead of selfishness. Jesus pours His grace and affection into us so that we can go and pour grace and affection into those around us. This is reciprocity the Jesus way.

### INDIVIDUALITY

Near the beginning of this lesson, you spotted some differences between Song of Songs 5:10–16, where the Shulammite praises her Lover's features, and Song of Songs 4:1–7, where he lists her stellar qualities. No doubt you noticed the similarities, but you probably also noticed that some of the most vibrant phrases in chapter 5 are very different from those in chapter 4, particularly the phrases concerning strength and beauty. While each Lover has some qualities of strength and some qualities of delicacy, the balance is clearly tipped on the scale for each of them in one area or the other.

Clearly, they are unique. One is a man, one is a woman. One is praised primarily for his strength, and the other, primarily for her beauty and flawlessness. God has given each distinctness, in their maleness and femaleness, as well as their own personalities, or personhood.

Which words speak of strength in chapters 4 and 5?

**STRENGTH**
The qualities or capacity of a person or thing to sustain or endure; intensity of belief; related to power, energy, and abilities

**DELICACY**
Very fine or intricate, requiring careful handling; particularly pleasing and special in various ways

Go back and underline those things you listed above that are attributed to the Shulammite woman, and circle those things that are attributed to Solomon, the male Lover. Your lists and circles and underlines may look different from mine, but are you getting a clear biblical sense that the scales are uneven?

Each member has strength, but this is a *primary quality for him*:

The Shulammite

- Her neck is like the tower of David (4:4).

Solomon

- He is ruddy (5:10).
- His arms are rods (5:14).
- His body is polished ivory (5:14).
- His legs are alabaster columns (5:15).

Each member is delicate, but this is a *primary quality for her*:

The Shulammite

- Her teeth are like a flock of shorn ewes (4:2).
- Her lips are like a scarlet thread (4:3).
- Her cheeks are like pomegranate halves (4:3).
- Her breasts are like two fawns (4:5).

Solomon

- His hair is fine gold (5:11).

We could easily be offended by categorizing and organizing traits of men and women, but then we would miss the insights Scripture has for us in our natures as men and women. I am not saying one is better than the other, or that qualities of masculinity and femininity don't overlap, but working through these differences helps us to rejoice in who God made us to be as women, rather than constantly searching for accolades intended for man.

God has clothed women with strength *and* dignity in Christ (Proverbs 31:25). Women of the Old and New Testaments, as well as modern women, have taken care of homes and families, protected themselves and loved ones from warfare and evil, stood up for what they believed in, and led armies real and metaphoric. Even in our delicacy, given as a gift from God, we can stand tall and strong. When we lead, it may look different from a male leading. When we choose to submit or follow rather than lead, we do so knowing the honor granted to us in that—the strength and delicacy intertwined in both leading and stepping back.

This concept of embracing both the strength and delicacy of our own sex is a countercultural idea.

# YOU SEE, IN A VERY BROAD SENSE, BECAUSE OF CHRIST, WE CAN DO EVERYTHING A MAN CAN DO, AND THEY CAN DO EVERYTHING THAT WE CAN DO (GALATIANS 3:28), BUT WE DON'T *NEED* TO.

We can embrace our created selves as male and female and stand across from each other, as the Lovers in Song of Songs do, extolling the gift of our similarities and our differences:

> "Look at him and how God made him. He is wonderfully male."
> "Look at her and how God made her. She is wonderfully female."

In understanding this, we then understand the complementary aspects of relationship. Because God created us male and female, we each have strengths to share in our relationships. Relationships between the sexes are complementary rather than competitive. I don't need to be the one to fill every need or receive every acknowledgment. God created each of us, whether male or female, different for a purpose. And Christ fills every void. He alone can be all things to all people, in a way that no one else can be for me in my life.

In the male and female relationships that we have, we learn and grow in Him because of our need for one another. We are complete, yet incomplete; strong, yet in need of one another's strength; delicate, yet needing one another's fragility to fully know Christ. The individuality and the reciprocity of how God has created relationships is crazily altogether beautiful.

## Inscribed upon My Heart

Use the Scripture memory verse for the week and the prayer prompt to bring your confession, thanksgiving, praise, and requests before the God who calls you beautiful.

### WEEK 5 MEMORY VERSE

"What is your beloved more than another beloved, O most beautiful among women? What is your beloved more than another beloved, that you thus adjure us?" Song of Songs 5:9

### PRAYER PROMPT

Father, thank You for making me unique in my characteristics of strength and delicacy . . .

# You Don't Need to Make Yourself Pretty for God

One of the most common phrases I hear from people about why they avoid church is this: "I have to get myself together first, then I'll get right with God." This belief demonstrates a misunderstanding of who God is. It comes from a culture that likes things put together and pretty. But God is a God who isn't afraid of messy and is oftentimes found in the mess. Christ Jesus didn't avoid the pain and suffering around Him; He walked into the midst of those in need of healing. He didn't shirk the torment of the cross; He willingly walked into the mess of death for our benefit. In all of His perfection, He willingly offers Himself to bring hope and order to our mess.

We will never be "ready" to present ourselves to God if we try to be less messy. Life is messy. People are messy. Sin is messy, and we are steeped in it from birth. Psalm 103:2–5 holds words of truth and hope:

> "Bless the LORD, O my soul,
>
> and forget not all His benefits,
>
> who forgives all your iniquity,
>
> who heals all your diseases,
>
> who redeems your life
>  from the pit,
>
> who crowns you with steadfast
>  love and mercy,
>
> who satisfies you with good
>
> so that your youth is renewed
>  like the eagle's."

He redeems us from the pit. We cannot crawl out of the pit of sin and life's darkness by ourselves. We could never get prettied up and be "ready" for Him to forgive us. We were and we are in the pit of our own sinfulness—by nature and by choice. But Jesus reaches into that pit, pulls us up by the power of the cross, lifts us to Him in the resurrection, and gathers us to Him through the Spirit. He does it again and again. He daily, hourly, continues to offer us love, affection, and mercy. We live forgiven and free.

Close your eyes with me and picture His hand, reached out, pulling you up from that pit, at your Baptism, and as you are now, today. God lifts us up and gathers us in His arms, thanks to the saving work that Christ has already done.

## GOD WANTS US TO BE AVAILABLE, BUT WE DON'T HAVE TO BE READY.

We can certainly make ourselves unavailable, like the ten virgins who run out to get oil for their lamps in the Gospels (Matthew 25:1–13). We easily run around and fret about all forms of things that just don't matter. We are distracted by life. We spend all kinds of time getting ready but being unavailable, trying to make our lives just so for God or for others. Only Christ makes ready.

You are redeemed from the pit.

It's not pretty, facing where we came from in our sin, but who needs pretty when Christ makes us *beautiful* in His love, His grace, and His redemption?

# Day 5

## OUR HELP
**SONG OF SONGS 6:1**

We all need people. For the most part, we all know this as fact. Have you ever tried to go it alone? I have. I remember when my first two children were very little. I had a two-year-old and a six-month-old. We lived in a new place, a new house, and were starting a new life at a new church. As one who easily made friends, I was surprised when friends didn't come so easily this time around. I suddenly found myself lonely and crawling more into my hole of aloneness every day. After several months of misery, I showed up at library story time determined to make a friend, one friend, despite the spit-up on my shoulder and the dark circles of sleepless nights under my eyes. And I did. She was a lot different than I expected, and she was wonderful. God knew exactly what He was doing in that season of my life, but it would have been a lot less painful for me had I embraced the fact earlier rather than later that I needed people.

In the midst of her crisis, the Beloved in Song of Songs 5 cries out in her need for people. If you open your Bible and skim back through chapter 5, you'll recall the cycle we just studied—she wakes to her Lover's knock, she doesn't want to get dressed, he leaves, she discovers she missed the opportunity to be with him, and she runs into the streets to seek out her Lover. In Song of Songs 5:8, she implores the Daughters of Jerusalem, whom we most commonly refer to as "the Others," to help her. Again, the Others' job is to give the Shulammite a platform on which to extol her lover. Her list in Song of Songs 5:10–16 is quite compelling, as we studied yesterday!

Today, we'll round out our study by examining the response from the Others in Song of Songs 6:1 and find some much-needed help for our Shulammite friend—and ourselves.

Please write out the response of the Others to the Shulammite's request for help, found in Song of Songs 6:1.

Helpful people always make me happy. When has a friend helped you out in a big or small way?

Help isn't always easy to come by. When in your life have you found yourself in need of help with no one to provide it? How did you deal with that situation?

Perhaps we don't always ask for help when we need it either, but the beauty of relationships that are centered on God is that they offer a unique sense of safety. Let's look at another biblical example of someone who needs help. God uses Moses' father-in-law, Jethro, to share some wisdom with Moses, who had a hard time asking for help.

Read Exodus 18:13–23. What was Moses' problem and Jethro's advice?

In asking for help, marvelous things happen. Jesus even invites us to ask for help (John 14:13–14). Upon His ascent into heaven, Jesus gave us the Holy Spirit to attend intimately to our groanings and needs. Then He did something really cool and created the Body of Christ, the Church, to help one another and to help a world in need.

The struggle comes, though, in discerning which voice we are hearing when we ask for help. Are we hearing the voice of the maker of the stars, the voice of idle worldly chatter, or the voice of the devil, who pushes nonsense into our lives?

How do we discern the voices of help from "the Others" in our own lives? How do you usually discern whether people's advice or instruction is helpful?

**Genesis 11:4**
"Then they said, 'Come, let us build ourselves a city and a tower with its top in the heavens, and let us make a name for ourselves, lest we be dispersed over the face of the whole earth.'"

The people in Genesis 11:1–9 decided to support one another on a venture. Please read this classic Bible story and share, in the space below, where you think this venture went wrong.

Where was the voice of reason in this story? The kind of help the people offered one another turned out to be no help at all. Did anyone, at any point, object to the harebrained idea of building a tower to reach the heavens?

If you had been there, how would you have offered help in the midst of teamwork gone bad?

Do you have any Others in your life who leave God out of the picture? What differences do you see there from your relationships that share belief in Christ?

These Others, whether your friends or family, may be important in your life, and rarely does God want us to throw relationships away, but firmer boundaries are necessary if they consistently leave God out of the picture in their own lives. The Others in our lives who do not know the Lord or often forget to add Him to the equation may not be the best people from whom to seek help when you need advice and discernment.

How else can Others in your life go terribly wrong? Look up the following verses. Beside each reference, write any unhealthy element in interpersonal relationships you can identify. Also write how each of these elements could have a negative impact on your relationship with God.

Matthew 24:10

Mark 9:34

Mark 9:50

The following verses give us some insight into relationships that build up. Read the passages below, and note how relationships are built up in the Lord.

Ecclesiastes 4:9–12

1 Thessalonians 4:9–12

John 13:34–35

I encourage you to fill your life, where you can, with others who build up. Who are those people in your life who help you establish good boundaries and encourage you in your relationship with God?

God's gift of relationship is one of the primary ways He continuously brings Himself into our lives. That's why all of our relationships are better surrounded by the Word of God. John 13:34–35, which you just read above, reminds us where the heart of all relationship sits—in our own most beautiful Savior, the lover of our souls, Jesus Christ. It's only through His love that we can begin to be a truly helpful Other to those around us. May our chorus and the chorus of our Others always be:

## "Where has your beloved turned, that we may seek him with you?" Song of Songs 6:1

May we always be ready to help those in our lives seek the One who loves their souls as well. Relationships that seek Jesus Christ in His Word and at His feet are altogether beautiful.

## Inscribed upon My Heart

Use the Scripture memory verse for the week and the prayer prompt to bring your confession, thanksgiving, praise, and requests before the God who calls you beautiful.

### WEEK 5 MEMORY VERSE

"What is your beloved more than another beloved, O most beautiful among women? What is your beloved more than another beloved, that you thus adjure us?" Song of Songs 5:9

### PRAYER PROMPT

Holy Spirit, thank You for each person You have put into my life. Guide my relationships . . .

# Week 6

WHAT A GLORIOUS GOD!

# Viewer Guide

## VIDEO 6: THAT WHICH IS TRULY AWESOME
### SONG OF SONGS 6:4–10

**VERSES TO BOOKMARK**
Song of Songs 6:4–10
Ephesians 6:10–12
Ephesians 5:25–30
Ephesians 5:20–24, 32

Today we are going to talk about things that are _____
_____.

תִּרְצָה אֲיֻמָּה

*Ayummah*: from the root word *ayom*, meaning "awesome, terrible, or dreadful." Fun fact: This word is pronounced "aw-yome," which even sounds similar to our English word *awesome*.

**TIRZAH AND JERUSALEM**
In Song of Songs 6:4–10, we see the inclusion of two locations that you will find on the map on page 7: Tirzah and Jerusalem. In Hebrew, *Tirzah* also means "delight," and Jerusalem is the royal city. These are compliments.[*]

## OUR AWESOME GOD

1. GOD'S _____ FOR US IS AWESOME.

Song of Songs 6:4:

"You are beautiful as Tirzah, my love,

    lovely as Jerusalem,

      awesome as an army with banners."

Song of Songs 6:10:

"Who is this who looks down like the dawn,

    beautiful as the moon, bright as the sun,

      awesome as an army with banners?"

The Bride is beautiful, but she is also ready _____ _____.

The everyday invisible spiritual warfare of God's people is *beautiful* to God.

2. CHRIST'S _____ IS AWESOME.

Christ gushes over His Bride by proclaiming what _____ has done for _____.

---

\* See Roland C. Ehlke, "Song of Songs," in *People's Bible Commentary* (St. Louis: Concordia Publishing House, 1992, 2004), 135–222.

The passage we just read from Ephesians 5 is ripe with Christ's affectionate action, which brings us salvation and restoration.

5:26: Christ affectionately _____ His Bride.

5:27: Christ _____ His Bride.

Ephesians 5:27 uses four gushing adjectives for what she—the Church—looks like to Him: "spotless," "wrinkleless," "without blemish," and "holy."

5:28–29: He loves the Church as His _____ _____.

5:29: He _____ His Bride.

He _____ His Bride.

3. _____ IS AWESOME.

One of the primary ways we show our affection for Christ is by
_____ to Him.

Christ's love for us makes the idea of submitting sweet _____
rather than harsh _____.

Submission is a response of love and trust. It is gushing affection shown to a God who loved us first.

Submission is rarely _____, but His love makes submission
_____.

## Discussion Questions

1. When you were growing up, what kind of affection did you see, hear, or receive in your household? How does Christ fill in the gaps of missing affection in our lives?

2. What is the hardest part of the idea of submitting for you?

3. Of the four adjectives found in Ephesians 5:27—"spotless," "wrinkleless," "without blemish," and "holy"—which one speaks to your heart the most as affection from Christ in the salvation He has won for you? Explain.

# Day 1

## THE GLORY OF GARDENS
## SONG OF SONGS 6:1–9

**SONG OF SONGS 6:5**
*"Turn away your eyes from me, for they overwhelm me."* There is a sense of terror in the Hebrew terminology; there is an unknown reason her eyes are almost frightening, maybe a testament to her power of influence over him, possibly translated as "they unsettle me" or "they drive me wild!"

**SONG OF SONGS 6:10**
*"Beautiful as the moon, bright as the sun."* She is glowing in her beauty; she radiates God's grace. She represents the Church, based on Revelation 12:1.

**SONG OF SONGS 7:4**
*"Your neck is like an ivory tower."* May refer to an actual tower in Jerusalem, or it possibly keeps with the military language and imagery of strength and dignity. Can be viewed from the list of features in the entire chapter list—feet, navel, breasts, belly—cited as a whole that she is a masterful creation of the Lord.

God, the master gardener, is always tending to His creation. He knows exactly what every plant needs, what microorganisms add the needed elements to the daily processes of growth and bearing fruit, and which birds and bees and critters bring energy and movement to the environment. He calls the sun to rise so His creation can grow. But as much as He cares for the natural world, our God cares for us even more!

"Consider the lilies, how they grow:
they neither toil nor spin, yet I tell you,
even Solomon in all his glory was not
arrayed like one of these." Luke 12:27

God speaks this message of love and affection loudly through the garden visits of the two Lovers in the Song of Songs.

Read Song of Songs 6:1–7. Identify any words about the garden in which the Lovers gathered together.

Identify any words or phrases that give a nod to moments of love and affection in that garden.

In this passage, Solomon and his bride meet together, come together in unity—in a pleasant place, in the garden—to tend to each other in love and mutual affection. Today, this would be like a husband and wife scheduling a leisurely date night, one that features lively conversation over a long dinner that includes an appetizer, salad, main course, dessert, and coffee. And it's only once the restaurant begins to turn out the lights that the couple realizes it's time to go home. The garden is time with less restraint than the daily stuff of life usually give us, a place where Solomon and his bride can completely focus on their relationship.

The togetherness of the Lovers in the garden also points us to the bigger picture of Christ and His Bride, the Church. God declares us His and we declare Him our great God. We could use the words of the Shulammite in Song of Songs 6:3 to describe the relationship with Christ and His Bride.

Write the words of Song of Songs 6:3 below.

God's plan since the creation of the world follows a garden path of love and care, from the moment of light's creation in the Garden of Eden to the redemption of the world in the empty garden tomb and on to the tree of life in the blessed restoration to come. Not unlike the garden to which Solomon and the Shulammite go, each garden in Scripture speaks to a deeper intimacy between God and His people, even in the difficult times.

Let's walk through Scripture together, from the creation to our redemption and finally to the restoration, to see a broader application of the garden in the Song of Songs for today.

## CREATION

Adam and Eve were created and were given the Garden of Eden to tend and care for together. They lived in peace and harmony. But the crafty serpent used his lies and twisted God's promises to tempt Eve, who fell into sin and brought her husband along for the ride. But before humanity's fall into sin, there was Genesis 3:6–13. The details in this passage speak to the intimacy that Adam and Eve were able to experience with God in that first garden.

Read Genesis 3:6–13. List details about the garden itself and life in the garden.

"They knew that they were naked" (v. 7). Adam and Eve lived together in nakedness before each other and before God. Little speaks of intimacy like nudity. Surprisingly, a huge part of the fall into sin involved clothing.

To understand this better, write Genesis 2:25 below.

When God created Adam and Eve and married them together, He intended for them to share everything with Him and with each other, to share everything in His creation with no shame. Solomon and the Shulammite's moments of adoration and affection in the garden in chapter 6 of the Song bespeak this time that our hearts all long for—the time when humanity experienced no shame, the time in the Garden of Eden before sin entered the world.

When sin entered into the world, however, relationships were the first thing affected, and not just married relationships but every relationship. Adam and Eve were suddenly aware of their nakedness. They became conscious of imperfection and of not being able to meet the standards of God and the new expectations of each other, for fulfillment and for grace, which only God can provide. Enter clothing, a cover-up.

The link between nudity and shamelessness we see in Genesis 2:25 resonates in Song of Songs 6–7. Glance ahead, skimming chapter 7. As Solomon notes the beauty of his wife's body, you will note the language of nakedness with no shame. How do you imagine this concept of nudity in body and spirit and shamelessness can be applied to the relationship between Christ and the Church today and in the perfect restoration to come?

The Body of Christ was created by God, not man. While it is imperfect, I believe God gave it to us as a gardenlike place in the midst of the struggles of this world—a place to meet with God, meet with His people, and rest, naked and unashamed; a place to just be ourselves.

Even though we have sinned and fallen short and the Church is imperfect, God still treasures us, sees us in our nakedness, and loves us anyway because of Christ Jesus. Thank goodness for our next section—redemption.

REDEMPTION

There are three references to gardens in Scripture particular to the week Jesus journeyed to the cross for our sake.

Read the following passages in order, and note next to the reference the events that transpired in each garden. Identify any words or actions of intimacy and affection that you find.

| EVENT | INTIMACY/AFFECTION |
|---|---|
| Matthew 26:36–45 | |
| John 18:1–11 | |
| John 19:41–20:1 | |

Good Friday sadness turned to resurrection joy! The tomb found within the garden was empty. He was not there. He had risen, just as He said He would!

The shamelessness that the Lovers desire for their relationship in the Song of Songs can only really be experienced through the death and resurrection of Jesus Christ, our Savior—He who takes all of our shame away.

But wait . . . what about all the shame and struggle today? What about the Church's imperfections and our own imperfections? Well, we are not done. We long for *complete* restoration.

## RESTORATION

By Song of Songs 6, we have seen Solomon and the Shulammite in the good, the bad, and the ugly. They are real and tangible people to us in their joys and their trials; when we examine their lives, we realize they are not so different from us today as we experience our own joys and sorrows. You'll find this joy and struggle intermingled clearly for our Shulammite in Song of Songs 6:8-9.

What is wonderful about the queen's life with her king identified here?

What is the queen's difficult daily reality told to us in Song of Songs 6:8?

Solomon was far from faithful. While God may have allowed for more than one wife in this Old Testament context (and that is surely debated among scholars!), remember that He warned Solomon against taking foreign wives, against yoking himself to women who would lead him to idolatry. You can read more on this in the article found on page 185. Can you imagine being wife number 1 of 60? Can your heart even venture longing for a husband's attention with 140-plus other women to contend with? I am sure that the Shulammite, while knowing God's mercy through the Word and sacrifices at the temple, longed for a more complete restoration, as we all do, with no more tears to cry into her pillow.

Please turn with me to Revelation 22:1–5. What throwback from the original Garden of Eden can you find?

Restoration doesn't ignore the past. Jesus' story is still told in the Book of Revelation. He is still the Lamb who was slain, but He stands ascended and triumphant. The tree of the knowledge of good and evil has no place in heaven. There are no serpents lurking to deceive us. We will literally walk with God again, in our nakedness without shame, singing with the angels, concerned only with His glory.

## "The leaves of the tree were for the healing of the nations." Revelation 22:2

Our healing and complete restoration in His garden is altogether beautiful.

### INSCRIBED UPON MY HEART

**ABOUT THIS VERSE**
God is a glorious God of creation, redemption, and restoration. He calls us His children, His precious treasure. He knows us in our deepest places, and we grow in intimacy with Him through faith in Jesus Christ, His Son, and around His Word.

Use the Scripture memory verse for the week and the prayer prompt to bring your confession, thanksgiving, praise, and requests before the God who calls you beautiful.

### WEEK 6 MEMORY VERSE
"I am my beloved's, and his desire is for me." Song of Songs 7:10

### PRAYER PROMPT
Lord Jesus, You invite us to intimacy with You through Your death and resurrection . . .

# Solomon's Downfall

Song of Songs 6:8–9 introduces into our pleasant story of two young newlyweds the downfall of a king.

## "Sixty queens and eighty concubines, and virgins without number"

Unfortunately, the Shulammite was not Solomon's only bride. The story is told in 1 Kings 11, and it will break your heart:

"Now King Solomon loved many foreign women, along with the daughter of Pharaoh: Moabite, Ammonite, Edomite, Sidonian, and Hittite women, from the nations concerning which the LORD had said to the people of Israel, 'You shall not enter into marriage with them, neither shall they with you, for surely they will turn away your heart after their gods.' Solomon clung to these in love. He had 700 wives, who were princesses, and 300 concubines. And his wives turned away his heart. For when Solomon was old his wives turned away his heart after other gods, and his heart was not wholly true to the LORD his God, as was the heart of David his father" (vv. 1–4).

This reality is really sad for us as we study this beautiful book—the Song of Songs. It's painful, really. Built into this train wreck, however, is also a great reminder: no one is perfect, no, not one, save Christ Jesus, our Lord. Romans 5:6 reminds us:

## "For while we were still weak, at the right time Christ died for the ungodly."

The Shulammite's testimony is not perfection. Solomon's testimony is not perfection. Christ's testimony shines brightest in our weakness. Song of Songs 6:8–9 reminds us that heroes are only as valuable as the one to whom they point us. Christ alone provides everything we need. Christ alone is perfect salvation for our souls. Only through Christ's sacrifice can we come to a holy and perfect God, whether we are a great and mighty king like Solomon or a lowly shepherdess in the fields.

While God forgives us in Christ when we confess our sins, we could save ourselves a whole lot of heartache by examining our heart in light of the Word of God, early and often.

What kinds of things entice us away from God? A few examples would be our plans, our ideas, our stuff, our relationships—things that are good but things that should never become our god.

As women, we can also poorly influence our husbands, our brothers, our friends, and our sons, as Solomon allowed his many wives to influence him. As women, we often like our timelines, our ways of spending money, our plans, our vantage points. Wives especially hold a special power of influence over their husbands. We can influence with demands and manipulation, or we can influence with encouragement and honor. Our influence can be a God-given gift when it is used to build up the leaders of our households, of our churches, and of our world.

Just some food for thought: In what ways do we push and push for our own desires and end up leading them away from God rather than closer to Him? In what ways can we as women spiritually encourage our husbands, our fathers, our brothers, our sons, or the men in our churches?

*Dear Lord, let our plans, our paths, and our people always return us to You—our great God and Lord. In Jesus' name. Amen.*

# Day 2

## THE GLORY OF CHRIST
### SONG OF SONGS 6:10–13

**MAKING CONNECTIONS**
Compare Solomon's compliment to his bride in 6:10 with what the Shulammite said about herself in 1:6! She saw herself as too dark, not beautiful enough, but her husband and her God see her as so much more. They say she is "as beautiful as the moon, bright as the sun, awesome."

In Song of Songs 6:10, we find perhaps the most extravagant compliment for Solomon's bride. I would dare to say this particular compliment surpasses any other compliment we find in the book. Of course, this is entirely subjective. Glance through the three translations below and write your own interpretation of Solomon's edification for his bride. (We aren't looking for Hebrew scholarship here, unless you feel so led.)

"Who is this who looks down like the dawn,
beautiful as the moon, bright as the sun,
awesome as an army with banners?" (ESV)

"Who is this that appears like the dawn,
fair as the moon, bright as the sun,
majestic as the stars in procession?" (NIV)

"Who is this that grows like the dawn,
As beautiful as the full moon,
As pure as the sun,
As awesome as an army with banners?" (NASB)

Write your own translation of Song of Songs 6:10 below.

I wish I could read every one of your thoughts! If I could choose a word to sum up Solomon's compliments to his wife in Song of Songs 6:10, I would use the word *radiant*.

The sun, the moon, and the stars pale in comparison with the beauty that stands before Solomon. It is no mistake that commentators remind us almost universally that whatever Solomon is or does, whatever the Shulammite is or does, they are only a small example of the glory of Christ Jesus.

Jesus affirms that He is greater than Solomon, or any man or woman, in Luke 11:31. At first glance, this may seem like a cryptic verse. Use Matthew 12:6–8 to help you decipher Jesus' language. Who is the one "greater than Solomon"?

**LUKE 11:31**
"The queen of the South will rise up at the judgment with the men of this generation and condemn them, for she came from the ends of the earth to hear the wisdom of Solomon, and behold, something greater than Solomon is here."

All glory on this earth, in the end, belongs to the glorious Son.

You may have no one around you calling you radiant, as Solomon does his bride, but I assure you, you are. Your radiance comes from the one who far surpasses anyone in all creation, Christ Himself. Hebrews 1:1–3 tells us about the flow of radiance in the kingdom of God, and Philippians 2:13–16 helps us to understand our place in it.

Read both Hebrews 1:1–3 and Philippians 2:13–16 to fill in the small flow chart below.

_____ → _____ → us

We may not feel so radiant most days. We may feel like everyone else is more interesting, more beautiful, smarter, more thoughtful, you name it. But the reality is, God has made each of us special by putting His Son in our hearts. The Spirit residing in us is true radiance, true beauty. When we trap ourselves in the comparison game of who's the most special, we rob ourselves of the knowledge and assurance of where any specialness comes from at all.

The Bible also tells us that we are radiant collectively as the Body of Christ.

Read Revelation 12:1. What heavenly bodies do you find represented in this verse that were also referenced in Song of Songs 6:10?

One thing about the Book of Revelation is that it requires some expert commentating. Most of the book is extremely figurative. If you think the language of pomegranates and goat's hair is intimidating in the Song of Songs, try the language of dragons and diadems in Revelation. My Bible's study notes give a little more insight into the meaning of Revelation 12:1: the "woman represents God's people (Israel and the Church), the saints of all times."[40]

Good to know. I would have missed that entirely.

Or would we have? Small passages like Song of Songs 6:10 help us to see how Scripture agrees with itself. We know now that God calls His people—His Bride, the Church—radiant. Can you see how the Scripture passages fit together beautifully, from our obscure book in the Old Testament (Song of Songs) to the vision of Revelation? Not one piece of God's message is lost in His Word.

There's another beautiful piece to our radiance in Christ, but we need to back up to see it. Read Song of Songs 6:9 below, and fill in the missing words to help make this whole radiance concept more concrete in our brains.

My dove, my perfect one, is the only one,

the only one of her mother,

pure to her who bore her.

The young women saw her and _____

_____  _____;

the queens and concubines also, and they _____...

_____.

We so often seek blessing. We want praise.

What do you think people believe makes a woman blessed?

If you listed kindness, a healthy family, friendships, or the like, you would be correct. These kinds of things are often what people believe make a woman blessed.

Biblically, though, *blessed* is a very different thing. In his Commentary of the Song of Songs, Mitchell shares his knowledge about blessing in the Old Testament: "[Old Testament] blessings in which people bless other people are declarative conferrals of God's grace—a benediction akin to absolution."[41] His insight changes the shape of how we see blessing in our lives today. Blessing in this sense is conferred by God on us and by proclaiming what we see God doing, how we see His grace working, in one another.

Solomon and the women in Song of Songs 6:9 do not call the Shulammite blessed because she is physically beautiful, because she is married to the king, because she has great fertility, or for any other tangible reason.

# THE PEOPLE CALL HER BLESSED BECAUSE GOD CALLS HER HIS.

The young women and the other queens and concubines represented in Song of Songs 6:9 are reminded of God's glory through her. As impossible as it seems to us, they proclaim His great conferral of grace and forgiveness on His people through their adulation of the Shulammite bride.

Who calls you blessed in your life? Who reminds you of the truth that you are God's child, loved and forgiven?

Whom do you lift up and affirm, conferring this honor and blessing on his or her life?

Who in your life needs to know there is a God who calls them beautiful because they are His? Who needs to know their specialness can only come from a God who wrote their names in His book at the creation of the world? May we always tell others of their specialness, bestowed by the Son, and rest secure knowing that He has a place for us too. That is altogether beautiful.

## INSCRIBED UPON MY HEART

Use the Scripture memory verse for the week and the prayer prompt to bring your confession, thanksgiving, praise, and requests before the God who calls you beautiful.

### WEEK 6 MEMORY VERSE

"I am my beloved's, and his desire is for me." Song of Songs 7:10

### PRAYER PROMPT

Lord, use me to bestow Your blessing of grace and forgiveness on those around me, especially . . .

# Day 3

## THE GLORY OF GROWTH
**SONG OF SONGS 7:1–9**

We made it to chapter 7 of the Song of Songs. You are doing great, digging in and finding all those treasures in Scripture along the way. Well done.

Do you blush easily? I do not, except when crushes, love, and relationships are concerned. In college, I watched a hunky baseball player, dressed in full uniform, saunter across the cafeteria; I was sure he was going to finally ask me out. I was ready and waiting, flashing a smile of expectation to my roommate, who stood nearby. Imagine my surprise when he asked me how he should ask *some other girl out*. There was a fair amount of blushing and excusing myself going on.

Thankfully, God's plans are grander. Two years later, I promptly married that hunky baseball player.

Share an instance in your life when you have blushed pink from embarrassment!

In Song of Songs 7:1–9, we read more of Solomon's affections that he poured out on his lovely queen. He speaks eloquently, of course, and this time his praises are more intimate than ever—enough to make a grown girl blush! It's helpful to remember the purpose of these soliloquies: Solomon sees the Shulammite as his flawless wife—a perfect complement to him—and telling her that is appropriate!

Through the lens of Christ, God sees us in the same way—complete and flawless, His perfect children, forgiven and made whole. It's appropriate for Him to proclaim these truths over us, especially while we live in a world where we will hear a million other false messages about who we are and whose we are.

What so far has been the most memorable message for you from the Song of Songs?

Every single message we read in Scripture points directly to Christ. God the Father also weaves His Word in such a way that what any of us remembers about each verse and passage on any given day speaks to each of our hearts very differently. Through the Holy Spirit's pen, men wrote the Word of God, including these words of Solomon in Song of Songs 7. God decided what the words would be then, and today He opens your heart to the individual nuance He wants *you* to hear and understand for your life and salvation today. We will continue to have our ears attuned to His Word in the Song of Songs for just a few more days, but may we always be open to the truth of His Word throughout all the days of our lives.

Please read today's text, Song of Songs 7:1–9. Name two images Solomon uses to describe his bride that jump out at you.

There are so many! One image that jumps out to me is the palm tree. It is repeated twice in verses 6–9. What do you know about palm trees? What makes a palm tree different from other trees?

One winter, my husband and I took a trip to Phoenix and slipped in a visit to the Desert Botanical Garden. I did not have high hopes. A desert . . . how interesting could that be? I wondered if we had fallen prey to the overly enthusiastic hotel manager's recommendation. But the desert gardens were beautiful! All you desert dwellers and wannabe desert dwellers will be happy to hear that I was definitely proven wrong by the entrance alone. I had no idea there were so many species of cactus. Plus, wow! I was floored by the variety of palm trees, and they were gorgeous—tall and stately palm trees; mini palm trees; fat, plump palm trees; palm trees that looked like the tops of pineapples; and palm trees that mimicked a skinny magic wand touching the sky. In Nebraska, the closest thing we have to palm trees are tumbleweeds and wildflowers—also spectacles of nature in themselves.

One thing I learned is that what sets the palm tree apart is its unique ability to survive in a low-moisture climate. It is a tree that is able to withstand the heat and still flourish. So when Solomon tells his bride, "Your stature is like a palm tree" (7:7), we realize what a compliment that is for our fair queen! She is one who is not easily bent, not easily harmed in the day of drought and struggle. In this passage, there are three things that set her and her relationship with Solomon apart from other women and other relationships that aren't growing in the same way.

1) She is tall and strong.

2) There is a clear presence of growth.

3) Together, Solomon and the Shulammite bear fruit in their relationship.

These three things can all be summed up in one word—*growth*. Being tall and strong and bearing fruit, as an individual or in a relationship, are visible elements of growth.

סַנְסִן

*sansin*: Hebrew root word for fruit stalk, specifically of the date palm[42]

Colossians 1:9–14 gives us a New Testament vantage point of these three concepts working together. Please read the passage and share what you learn about strength, growth, and bearing fruit.

Redemption and forgiveness bring light into our lives, much-needed light. We were once in darkness, dead in our sins, wilted, dried up, and parched. Can a plant get water for itself? Can a dead tree bring itself back to life? No. Plant life relies on the God of heaven and earth for sunshine, water, and growth, just like we do! We find our strength in Christ to stand strong and tall, to grow deep roots and live a colorful life that blooms and bears fruit. In our study of His Word and in our communion with the fellowship of all believers, we grow and thrive.

In the Song of Songs, the Lovers *tend* their relationship. They share their time and energy, put forth effort, and affirm each other. They grow together, strongly rooted, even when the climate is dry, the land is parched, and their relationship is less than stellar. Jesus' light shines into their relationship, and "the Daughters of Jerusalem," the witnesses around them, look on and proclaim it good and fruitful because they see visible growth, even in the imperfection.

This is how our relationship with God works. He tends. We receive. He sends us His Word written in ink. He gives us people to guide and support us. We tend to this relationship also. He sends the Holy Spirit so that we can respond and pick up His Word day in and day out, seeking His face. And the miracle of growth happens. Will there ever be drought? Yes. We will feel the parched and drying consequences of a sinful world, at some times more than others.

How have you seen growth occur in times of loss, times of struggle, or other "dry" times?

In times of struggle, how have you witnessed Christ's mercy in unexpected ways?

The beauty of authenticity is usually best seen in times of drought. When the world is pushing in on us, when we ache, we still turn to our great God to tend to us. We grow, and by His power others grow through it! That witness has so much power.

Fill in Ephesians 4:15–16 below.

"Rather, speaking the truth in love, we are to _____

_____ _____ _____ _____

into Him who is the head, _____ _____,

from whom the whole body, joined and held together by every

joint with which it is equipped, when each part is working properly,

_____ _____ _____

_____ so that it builds itself up in love."

We grow *into* something, or rather, someone—Christ. We are all on this journey together. Just like Solomon and the Shulammite are collaborative in the effort they put into their relationship, the collaborative relationship of the Body of Christ is an important part of the growth process.

In what ways would it be difficult to grow without other believers around you?

Next to the palm tree, write different ways God has provided for you to "grow into the head," which is Christ, and to grow with believers around you. These ways might include concrete things like daily devotions, or you might include people in your life, places you go, or verses that God has used to grow you up in Him.

Growth is such a funny thing too. Solomon and his bride were 100 percent married the moment they proclaimed their wedding vows to each other, but we see them growing deeper in their relationship every day. So we are in our relationship with Christ: 100 percent redeemed, justified, and set free in our Baptism, but growing deeper in our relationship with Him every day.

How is your relationship with Christ different today than it was at your Baptism?

You are His palm tree. Keep growing strong and tall through His Word, at His table, and with His people. Palm trees (who knew!) are altogether beautiful.

## Inscribed upon My Heart

How are you doing with the Scripture memory verse for the week? Scripture memory is one of those practices of tending to your relationship with God. You may not see the benefits immediately, but it impacts your heart over time, giving His strength when you need it. Use this verse and the prayer prompt to bring your confession, thanksgiving, praise, and requests before the God who calls you beautiful.

### WEEK 6 MEMORY VERSE
"I am my beloved's, and his desire is for me." Song of Songs 7:10

### PRAYER PROMPT
Lord, I praise You for Your work in my life. Help me to grow up through . . .

# Day 4

## THE GLORY OF KNOWING
### SONG OF SONGS 7:10; 2:16; 6:3

Our memory verse for the week, Song of Songs 7:10, is another tiny snippet of Scripture we might otherwise easily pass over. Maybe you have already committed it to memory. Let's test our skills.

Please write out Song of Songs 7:10 in the space below. If you don't have it memorized already, no worries; feel free to peek.

We have seen this language twice before in the Song. Look back at Song of Songs 2:16 and 6:3 to refresh your memory.

Looking at the three verses together, what is different in Song of Songs 7:10 from 2:16 and 6:3?

All of a sudden, in chapter 7, we have the added note of desire.

Does the word *desire* make the tips of your ears burn a little? Oftentimes, we subconsciously lump all desire into the category of temptation. And the special file folder in our brains that categorizes the word as such warns us to stomp desire way down or put the fire out before it gets the best of you.

God created desire in the very beginning. In week 3, we addressed the curse and Gospel of desire given in Genesis 3:16. I do not believe Satan's temptation and the subsequent curse are the entrance of desire into our world, but rather the curse begins humankind's *struggle* with desire entering our world. Our struggle with desire is a fruit of sin in the world coupled with desire. This form of desire becomes connected to temptation and fulfillment, searching and longing for something more, something better. But God uses desire to point us straight to our need for Christ Jesus.

In Genesis 4:1, we see another form of desire. Fill in the missing verbs in Genesis 4:1 below.

"Now Adam _____ Eve his wife, and she _____

and bore Cain, saying 'I _____ _____

a man with the help of the Lord.'"

This passage makes me happy. Let Eve's phrase roll off your tongue out loud: "I have gotten a man with the help of the Lord."

How many desires of your heart has God fulfilled? How many desires have you "gotten … with the help of the Lord"? Share one or a few of these with us.

All praise to Him! What desires of your heart have gone unfulfilled?

We do not always "get" the desires of our heart. It's hard. It can feel like God has forgotten us, like we are unworthy. But it's in times like these when we must stand in the truth of God's Word even more firmly. He is always listening to the desires of our hearts. He hears us as we pray to Him about the secret places of our hearts, and He values our prayers, no matter what His answers are to them.

One aspect of desire that might be intriguing to you is connected to the biblical word translated "know" in Genesis 4:1. Your Bible may read "knew," "made love," or "had relations." All of these could be considered accurate, but in our English translation we may miss the fullness of the word *knew* found in the original Hebrew, which is יָדַע, transliterated *yada*. This word is much fuller than sexual intimacy. Some of the definitions coming from this root word *yada* include:[43]

| | |
|---|---|
| • to acknowledge | • to perceive |
| • to make myself known | • to be found |
| • to know with clarity | • to take notice |
| • to learn | • to understand |

Obviously, context matters, but taking the entire context of the Bible into consideration, we can discern this:

# WE WERE MEANT TO KNOW.
# WE WERE CREATED TO KNOW.
# WE WERE CREATED TO BE KNOWN.

Let's discover more about knowing today in the context of three relationships in particular.

RELATIONSHIP NO. 1: BEING KNOWN BY A SPOUSE AND KNOWING A SPOUSE

Biblically, it is true that marriage is the most intimate that you can be with another human being. Before I go too much further, I'm sure some of you are asking, "Wait! What about me? I'm not married." It's important to clarify that singleness is also a gift of God. That sounds like a statement to make any girl roll her eyes, but the heart of it is this: you don't need a spouse to complete you.

# UNMARRIED LIFE IS NOT LESS OF A LIFE. MARRIED LIFE COMPARED WITH SINGLE LIFE IS A *DIFFERENT* LIFE.

Marriage between a man and a woman yields a literal "onefleshness" in a way no other relationship can. God intended for a husband and wife to emotionally know each other deeper than they know anyone else and to be more free with each other than anyone else to share their intimate thoughts and desires in the safety of the commitment of marriage. Single or married, we can learn about God and ourselves by talking about the uniqueness of knowing in the marriage relationship.

From your experience as a married person or as one who has witnessed marriages around you, what does it look like for a husband and wife to know each other, to really know each other?

After seventeen years of marriage, you would think it would be easy, that my husband and I might know everything there is to know about each other. But marriage isn't really like that. Growing together is knowing my husband more each day. This means being vulnerable. It's a little like major surgery, cutting out all the ugly bits we don't really want others to see so that God can use us to tend to the deep places of each other's heart and soul. Sexuality is vulnerable, emotions are vulnerable, communicating with words and actions is vulnerable. But God designed marriage to be a place where husbands and wives can be safe in the vulnerability.

Read Matthew 1:18–21. How did Joseph open himself up to vulnerability by simply remaining as Mary's husband?

## "[He was] unwilling to put her to shame."
Matthew 1:19

Joseph displayed one level of intimacy by looking to divorce Mary quietly, to honor her, even though he believed she had sinned. Yet, he acknowledged her struggle and acted in grace, offering a level of safety and care many other men might not have been so willing to offer. Then, through the miracle of an angel sent by God, Joseph heard a message of almost unthinkable mercy (Matthew 1:18–25) and acquiesced to become even more vulnerable: *Mary's shame would become his own, or at the very least, it would be a shared shame.*

The world around Mary and Joseph—their family, friends, and neigh-bors—did not know the truth. Most of them were ignorant of God's plan and timing. Yet Mary and Joseph together bore the weight of God's call. He gave them the gift of each other to walk that road, just as the Shulammite walked alongside Solomon as he ruled a kingdom and just as we support and care for our husbands and friendships through thick and thin today.

RELATIONSHIP NO. 2: KNOWN BY THE BODY AND KNOWING THE BODY

Turn to 1 Corinthians 12:12–26. What sticks out to you most about the design of the Body of Christ? Maybe a word or a section jumps off the page at you.

Saying "I need you" is the beginning of intimacy. Why is it vulnerable to "need" another? In what ways is this hard, even within the Body of Christ?

For those of us who are super independent, it may take a little more effort to let the Body in. Living as part of the Body helps us to hold tight to the one true faith, to extend grace when it's difficult, and to lift up the cross when the world would want us to trample it underfoot. We were meant to be known and to know others in the Body of Christ.

How well do you know those in your local church? Is there any way that you could be plugged in more, extend a little more vulnerability?

The Book of 1 Corinthians also says that God gives greater honor to those who are weaker (12:22). Isn't that just like Jesus, to show honor and lift up those who are struggling the most?

Ephesians 4:15–16 gives insight into how we can honor one another. Underline what and how we speak according to these verses, printed below.

"Rather, speaking the truth in love, we are to grow up in every way into Him who is the head, into Christ, from whom the whole body, joined and held together by every joint with which it is equipped, when each part is working properly, makes the body grow so that it builds itself up in love."

We speak truth with love, and we speak love with truth, and God does His work. We are able to confess our sins and receive absolution. In the same way, we are able to receive someone else's confession and offer them absolution. In the Body, we have a place to be vulnerable and to share our own vulnerabilities, the times we've messed up, the ways in which we are currently struggling.

In 1 Corinthians 12:26, Paul writes that if one person is honored, we rejoice together, but also if one person suffers, we all suffer. How have you shared the burden of another member of the Body by suffering alongside him or her, helping by walking with him or her through a difficult time?

When have you received the gift of rejoicing with someone in the Body? Share about that as well!

RELATIONSHIP NO. 3: KNOWN BY CHRIST AND KNOWING CHRIST

I pray that you heard the two sections above as sweet Gospel. Being known and knowing others in this life surely is bittersweet. Whatever people can do for us, Christ does more. Christ gives more. Christ is more. There is nothing as sweet in life as knowing and being known by the Lamb of God.

Read Philippians 3:3–10. On the chart below, list all the reasons Paul has to boast in himself on the left-hand side. On the other side, write some of your own accomplishments, even those you look forward to in the future, God willing—like having children or going back to school.

| Paul's boasts | My boasts |
| --- | --- |
|  |  |

Now, write the word *rubbish* across your list. It's a bit painful, isn't it? But it's purposeful.

Write Philippians 3:10 below.

To know Christ is everything. To know Him more deeply through His Word and through the Spirit living and breathing in us—that's the sweetest knowing of all. We can know success, we can know our children, we can know friends, we can know so much stuff, but being known by Christ, being in a relationship with our precious Lord and Savior? *That* is altogether beautiful.

# Inscribed upon My Heart

Use the Scripture memory verse for the week and the prayer prompt to bring your confession, thanksgiving, praise, and requests before the God who calls you beautiful.

## WEEK 6 MEMORY VERSE

"I am my beloved's, and his desire is for me." Song of Songs 7:10

## PRAYER PROMPT

Lord, You hear the desires of my heart, both fulfilled and seemingly unfulfilled . . .

# Day 5

## THE GLORY OF FRUIT
### SONG OF SONGS 7:10–13

For one year of our early married life, my husband worked at a winery. It was a beautiful place, atop Missouri limestone bluffs, overlooking rolling hills filled to the brim with vines of plump grapes of all different varieties. In late September came the harvest. I remember for the employees there was a lot of work, a lot of sweat, long hours, and bugs, but at the end of it the owner of the vineyard threw a harvest party. Dave and I dressed in our fancies, dropped the kiddos with the grandparents, and had ourselves one of the best date nights on record in human history. There was singing and dancing, food and drinks, laughing, and so much joy you could feel it on your skin.

The joy struck me the most. People weren't over-the-top joyful because they indulged in too much wine or because of the feast of food or because of other tangible pieces to the party. They were filled with joy, it seemed to me, because of a job well done; the season had included hard work, uncertainty, and changes in plans, but it all came to fruition.

What a perfect picture of relationships and marriage in particular! The people in our lives are lots of work; communication is rarely spot-on; there are bugs to be worked out in plans and ideas. In marriage, the dailyness of the work, whether frustrating or joyful, can be so overwhelming that you miss the moments when the harvest rolls around, but it does roll around.

Our Lovers in the Song of Songs get a harvest moment in Song of Songs 7:10–13. They are given a moment to really celebrate their love together, to be intimate in the fullest sense of the word. The language of belonging in verse 10 illuminates a reminder of their married state in this portion of the Song.

Because it's our memory verse for the week, let's take the opportunity to write Song of Songs 7:10 below.

It is by no means an accident that the Lovers find themselves in the vineyard for building intimacy. When we use Scripture to interpret Scripture, we see the myriad ways vineyards consistently speak of deep intimacy.

### A NOTE FOR MARRIED WOMEN

Marriage beds are meant to build intimacy and celebrate the "harvest" of married life together. It's so easy to want to look past the sexual tension and desire found in the Song of Songs, but even this has a practical as well as a theological purpose in Scripture. Take a tip from the Lovers of the Song of Songs: Celebrate a harvest of passion with your husband and give some love. Eagerly prepare for the marriage bed. It will go well for you. It brings choice fruit. Lay up some time for your beloved that only you can give him.

Please read Song of Songs 7:10–13 again, and note below all the language associated with vineyards in this segment of Scripture.

One of my favorite passages about vineyards is found in John 15:1–9. Read that passage. What does Jesus teach us about vineyards in these verses?

John 15:4 tells us that we can do nothing without Christ. Putting these verses together with Song of Songs 7:10–13, we begin to ask ourselves this question: Why would we want to do anything without Christ anyway? The Shulammite's vantage point reminds us that the Beloved, the vine, is the source of nutrition, solidarity, and strength for each branch. In our relationship with Jesus, this is even more true. Where would we be without Him? In Him we produce good fruit, a harvest.

Sometimes we begin the mental game of berating ourselves for not producing:

"I'm not really that committed."

"I have so far to go in my faith."

"Fruit? I don't see it."

But when we put together our Song of Songs passage with John 15, we begin to get a greater understanding that while fruit may look like evangelism and discipleship, in these verses it looks mostly like simple relationship. God brings us close to Him, and we are part of His vineyard. Our relationship with God is the most precious fruit of the harvest. We don't need to berate ourselves for the fruit we do not see. He sees it. Our job is to tuck in closer to the Vine, which is Christ Jesus.

Jesus gives us physical testimony to our intimacy with Him, our relationship with Him, by using the very fruit of the vine from in the verses we have been studying today. Jesus chooses simple grapes to give us Himself in the Lord's Supper.

Read Matthew 26:17–30. What two elements did Jesus offer and share with His disciples in His Last Supper?

## "And He took a cup." Matthew 26:27

On the cross, Jesus physically sacrificed Himself for our forgiveness, our redemption, our justification, but He also continuously offers His physical presence through the bread and wine at the Communion Table. When He instituted the Lord's Supper, Jesus didn't say, "This bread symbolizes My body and this wine symbolizes My blood." In His Supper, He gives His very self to us. He said, "'Take, eat; this *is* My body.' And He took a cup, and when He had given thanks He gave it to them, saying, 'Drink of it, all of you, for this *is* My blood of the covenant, which is poured out for many *for the forgiveness of sins*'" (Matthew 26:27–28, emphasis added). When we gather with the Body of Christ and hear His words and share in eating and drinking these elements together, we give testimony to Him and who He is and we receive forgiveness anew. How is it that Christ continues to give us so much? John 15:9 gives us this answer and identifies the thread we see throughout Scripture—from the Song of Songs to the Last Supper of our Lord, shared within the Church of the New Testament, to the Body of Christ lifting the cup of His true blood today.

Fill in the missing words from John 15:9 below.

"As the Father has _____ Me, so have I _____ you.

Abide in My _____."

Love in our homes shown in physical affection, love in our churches shared around a physically present Vine . . . isn't it altogether beautiful?

**LIVING IN THE MYSTERY**
So much of how God reveals Himself to us is a mystery. I'm constantly drawn back to Isaiah 55:8 on topics like the Lord's Supper, Baptism, and how the Trinity works: "For My thoughts are not your thoughts, neither are your ways My ways, declares the LORD."
God's Word guides us in our belief, but it doesn't mean we'll understand it all. Sometimes we are called to live in the mystery. Think of it—bread and wine as body and blood; man and wife becoming one flesh; God's grace turning my sins white as snow through one man's crucifixion. These are beautiful, fabulous mysteries.

# INSCRIBED UPON MY HEART

Use the Scripture memory verse for the week and the prayer prompt to bring your confession, thanksgiving, praise, and requests before the God who calls you beautiful.

## WEEK 6 MEMORY VERSE

"I am my beloved's, and his desire is for me." Song of Songs 7:10

## PRAYER PROMPT

Lord, in Your Holy Spirit, let me love those around me today by . . .

# WEEK 7
## THE LANGUAGE OF ETERNITY

# Viewer Guide

VIDEO 7: A LOVE STRONGER THAN DEATH
**SONG OF SONGS 8:6–7**

**VERSES TO BOOKMARK**
Song of Songs 8:6–7
2 Timothy 2:19
Ephesians 1:13–14
Hebrews 12:2, 28–29

Song of Songs 8:6–7 brings to mind a few questions:

- Who has the right to be jealous over our lives and our hearts?
- Is jealousy ever appropriate?
- Is God a jealous God?
- Does God have the right to be jealous for His people?

The Song of Songs, in the context of all of Scripture, can give us insight into these very difficult questions, for our romantic lives and our spiritual lives.

## THE SEAL AND THE FLAME

The seal helps us understand _____ identity and _____ plan for our life.

The flame helps us to understand _____ identity and

His _____ as Lord and Savior.

It helps to look at Song of Songs 8:6–7 in both the horizontal and vertical realms:

**Horizontal**: Scripture's message for our relationship with other people.

**Vertical**: Scripture's message for our relationship with God.

### THE SEAL
Song of Songs 8:6a:

"Set me as a seal upon your heart, as a seal upon your arm."

#### The Horizontal Realm

In Song of Songs 8:6–7, the Shulammite invites her husband to place his seal on her. This is her invitation for him to mark her as his own.

This is a _____ offering within the context of _____.

The Vertical Realm

God sets a seal on us that says, _____ _____ of God.

The seal is intimately connected with the _____ of _____.

SONG OF SONGS 6:3
"I am my beloved's and my beloved is mine."

Christ has set His seal on us, and so we bear the name of Christ, the name of the living God.

## THE FLAME

Song of Songs 8:6b:

"For love is strong as death,

jealousy is fierce as the grave.

Its flashes are flashes of fire,

the very flame of the LORD."

The Horizontal Realm*

Belonging is reserved for _____, even in our _____.

At its heart, the design of marriage is to proclaim God's passion and desire for oneness with His Church, His people, even when we mess it up.

The Vertical Realm

What exactly can we learn about God's jealousy through Song of Songs 8:6–7?

God's jealousy is grounded in _____ and desire for relationship with us.

קִנְאָה

qinah: ardor, zeal, jealousy, kindled by divine love**

## DISCUSSION QUESTIONS:

1. What kind of relationships have you been around that show a healthy belonging, centered in Christ?

2. What struggles, if any, do you have with understanding the jealousy of God?

3. What hope and encouragement do you have from the knowledge that God sets His seal on you in Baptism?

---

\*   Christopher W. Mitchell, *The Song of Songs*, Concordia Commentary, edited by Dean O. Wenthe (St. Louis: Concordia Publishing House, 2003), 1182.

\*\*  "Bible Hub Interlinear Bible," http://biblehub.com/hebrew/7068.htm, accessed on July 27, 2017.

# Day 1

One of my favorite couples in the world are Marv and Marcella. They are some of the coolest people I know. Well into their eighties, they have been married more than sixty-five years! Marv is a World War II veteran and a farmer, and he can fix just about anything in a house, barn, or field. A few years ago, I accidentally flushed a cloth diaper down the toilet (true story!) and who came to snake it out? Marv did. Sweet Marcella can spend hours telling you humorous and precious stories of a life lived well, of raising their eight children. They are ridiculously cute together, mostly because of the kindness that they constantly show to each other.

During a recent Valentine's Day dinner put on by our youth group, Marv and Marcella, as well as several other couples, participated in a game in which the moderator asked each couple what they argued about most frequently. Marv and Marcella looked at each other, perplexed. I can still hear Marv's voice as he shrugged and nonchalantly admitted, "You know, after so many years, I don't think there's anything left to argue about. It's just not worth it for the small time we have left together before God calls us home."

Marv and Marcella's love story isn't miraculously free from struggle. They have grieved the loss of a ten-month-old son, endured hardships and struggle alongside twenty-five-plus grandchildren and great-grandchildren, and are not immune to the sorrow of loved ones who have walked away from the Church.

## STRUGGLE DOESN'T END MARRIAGES, JUST LIKE HAPPINESS DOESN'T KEEP MARRIAGES GOING.

Sin is the real culprit, and not just any sin, but sin left alone, unacknowledged, left to fester and pour out into our homes and families. Marv and Marcella make a great couple and share a love that lasts not because they are perfect, but because they know they are forgiven. I would consider having a love story like theirs as a relationship goal for sure.

What are three things you would put on your personal list of relationship goals?

1)


2)


3)


Life is wonderful and life is hard. The Song of Songs does not leave the hard stuff of life out. It acknowledges the beauty of life and relationships, as well as the difficult stuff we, too, will always find in our relationships on this earth. Just as the Lovers find time for each other, the bride turns from her husband because she wasn't ready. They also have to acknowledge the influence of jaded brothers and aggressive watchmen in their relationship, and the many-wives thing throws a wrench in at some point, I'm sure. What sets the Song apart from what we normally find in romantic literature is not the beauty found in perfect communication and perfect relationship, but the Lovers' expressed desire to be with each other, come what may, and the deeper commitment, the perfect eternal commitment of Christ to His people.

Which struggle of the Lovers in the Song feels the most familiar to you or is easiest for you to relate to?




Which passages of the Song have been the most encouraging to you so far?




Chapter 8 of the Song of Songs finds the same Lovers as in chapter 1, still gushing their love for each other. Read Song of Songs 8:1–5, and list any words or actions that speak of love and affection.




You might think the Lovers were teenagers zealous for their new love, but we know from the context of the verses in the book as a whole that this part of the text is a picture of Solomon and the Shulammite after having been married for a length of time. Commentator Matthew Henry points out in reading the text that you can see that the Lovers love each other in chapter 8 as strongly as they do in chapter 1.[44] The Song of Songs teaches us an important principle as we look from the first chapter to the last—*love ages*.

Identify a relationship, romantic or otherwise, in which you were surprised by the depth of love and care shared over time, through good days and bad days.

### New Love and Seasoned Love

While love changes shape and looks different over time, new love is not more passionate than seasoned love, and seasoned love is not more devout than new love. Love is a journey, just as life is a journey.

A small physics lesson here might help us understand the nature of the journey. The second law of thermodynamics teaches that everything is in a state of growth or decay. This applies to the environment, but it also applies to relationships. In reality, there is no status quo, no stagnation in life. If we tend to our relationships, particularly in and through God's grace, we grow. If we do not tend to things, things slowly move toward death and decay. We do have a God of resurrection, and He's in the business of making broken and decaying things new and alive again, but we also live in a world where the reality is this: we can end up with a lot of heartache when we don't tend.

How would you explain this "growth and decay" concept, a concept at work in our world and our relationships, to a friend?

What kinds of things grow a relationship? Consider some positive things, like time spent together, as well as some difficult things, like conflict and forgiveness.

As always, the Bible has some wisdom for us. Read each of the following passages. Beside each one, write a way Christ brings growth into our lives through tending.

Proverbs 1:5


Ephesians 4:13–15


2 Thessalonians 1:3


2 Peter 3:18


Song of Songs 8:1–5 has a particular emphasis on home and family life. Read this passage again, and list any words or actions related to home and family life.


Look for more on these strange and vivid details tomorrow. For now, let's let this passage as a whole remind us that love, while found in many places and spaces, is learned and shared particularly in the form of family life. Whether you're single or married, you can appreciate that our primary way of understanding love is through the family unit, whether that's with our parents or our grandparents or another duct-taped-together, gift-given family. Even in the struggles and failings so many families experience, families have a major impact on how we understand and experience love.

What did your family of origin teach you about love, intentionally or unintentionally?


How does your relationship with your mother and/or father affect your view of God's love for you?

Our families are certainly not the only way God brings love to us. God uses His Word to tell us about His love for us, and He gives us visible signs of His love in the waters of Baptism and the bread and wine of the Lord's Supper. He also gives us the people of His Church to fill in where our families may not have provided everything we need. In fact, God knows our families can't provide everything we need—only He can give us everything. When we expect our families to give us everything we need, we will be sorely disappointed.

Remember, the Shulammite eventually had to share Solomon with many wives and concubines and children who weren't hers. Can you imagine the weight that brought to their marriage? What concerns or insecurities do you think the Shulammite may have had to deal with?

God does not leave just one person to bear the load of sharing love with us. God sends others into our lives to take part in the journey. This is one reason we continuously return to church with other believers to hear His Word. We are reminded often that we can run to Him in the good times and the difficult times.

Here's the coolest thing: God can restore *every* relationship. We know very little about the Shulammite and Solomon's relationship outside of the Song of Songs. However, we do know that God faithfully works in the brightest and the darkest places, no matter the age of love. Because God restores us to Himself in Christ Jesus—because God restores His Bride, the Church, even when she experiences quarrels and division—we know that He can restore anything.

Write God's promises of restoration beside each of the following passages.

Deuteronomy 30:1–4

Acts 3:17–21

God restores. He restores relationships when we *feel* like love is dying. He restores family when *everything* breaks apart. He restores pieces of our broken hearts and puts them back together with His unfailing love and affection, *no matter* the situation. Along our journey, God is always restoring, in His way, in His time. Whether He's doing a new thing or seasoning an old relationship with the salt of time and growth, He restores. Isn't it altogether beautiful?

## Inscribed upon My Heart

Use the Scripture memory verse for the week and the prayer prompt to bring your confession, thanksgiving, praise, and requests before the God who calls you beautiful.

### WEEK 7 MEMORY VERSE

"I am my beloved's, and his desire is for me. . . . Set me as a seal upon your heart, as a seal upon your arm, for love is strong as death, jealousy is fierce as the grave. Its flashes are flashes of fire, the very flame of the LORD." Song of Songs 7:10; 8:6

### PRAYER PROMPT

Redeemer, in all of the seasons of life, You are watching over and guiding us . . .

---

**ABOUT THIS VERSE**
God sets the seal of His Spirit on us at our Baptism, and He tends the flame of faith in us through His Word and fellowship with the Body of Christ. His love for us is fierce and strong. Jesus overcame the grave to bring us life!

# Day 2

## FOOD FOR AFFECTION
## SONG OF SONGS 8:1–5

My husband and I recently taught the concept of *small affections* to couples at our church's marriage retreat. A small affection might be a hand on the shoulder, a pat on the back, a kiss on the cheek, a quick hug, or maybe holding hands walking to the car. These very brief moments of attention let someone you care about know without words that you are attentive to them and value their presence. It's like *appropriate* PDA.

Small affections say, "I noticed you are here. I'm glad you're here in the midst of life." And small affections are appropriate for relationships other than marriage. For example, my mom is so good at small affections. We may be in a room full of people, but she will almost always touch my knee softly and say, "I'm so glad you're here." What a difference this small gesture makes!

During the time when the Song of Songs was written, about 970 BC, public displays of affection between couples were frowned on in Near East culture. Poetry and words of affection, however, were not. The female Beloved in the Song tells her Lover in Song of Songs 8:1–2 that she would love to be his sister. Why? Well, sisters and brothers, as well as parents, could show appropriate affection publicly in a way that Lovers could not.[45]

Read Song of Songs 8:1–2. Underline or jot down every verb or action word the Shulammite would apply to her Lover if they were family members.

Many verbs of affection are appropriate within the family unit! We often may only think of hugging or kissing as a small affection. We may even take affections for granted, affections like leading with wisdom, teaching around the table, bringing to and fro, and giving, whether food, time, patience, or love. The Shulammite widens our vision for intentional interactions with those in our lives. She delights in the very idea of having a multidimensional and very domestic relationship with her husband. I'll highlight three of those domestic affections for our lesson. Domesticity may seem mediocre and ordinary, but God works in the mediocre and ordinary.

Nursing is one of the most intimate experiences mothers can share with their children. It is not necessary for attachment, we know, but we also know that it aides in creating a strong bond between baby and mother. Attachment is not only a scientific concept with hormones and bonding chemicals involved, but it is also a theological concept. It can be frustrating for young mothers when nursing is a challenge. They desire the touch of their baby, just as much as the baby desires his or her mama. We were made for connection.

God created human beings to attach to one another, especially family members. He's the one who created hormones and dopamine and all the good stuff that aids in bonding and attachment. He also is the one who brings children into adopted homes and gives us uncles and aunts and grandparents who make up our village. He creates bonds between individuals who are not family by blood but are family in every other sense of the word. He works His plan for us to be connected and to connect in so many different ways.

In Isaiah 66:10–14, God proclaims the time of peace in Christ to come for the Israelites. Please read this passage. What images of care and parenting does God use to share the promise of salvation in this passage?

> **ISAIAH 66:12**
> "Behold, I will extend peace to her like a river, and the glory of the nations like an overflowing stream; and you shall nurse, you shall be carried upon her hip, and bounced upon her knees."

God is the source of every good thing. He uses the structure of family and the structure of church family to help us understand His great care and affection for us. Isaiah 66 shares the message of God showing mercy on His people, even though the Israelites had forsaken Him. This passage speaks of His grace poured out when He could have turned the other way. God, in Christ, gathers us to Him and holds us close to His chest, as a mother does. Isaiah reveals a closeness with our Savior that the Shulammite alludes to in Song of Songs 8 when she talks in terms of sharing the domestic life.

Just days before His death, Jesus mourns over a city, a people, that will crucify Him. Turn in your Bible to Luke 13:34, and write Jesus' lament below.

God has always longed for people to turn to Him. The Shulammite's longing for her Lover is only a shadow of God's desire to bring us into His house in heaven. He sends His Spirit that we may come to Him. Through Christ, we receive the fulfillment of "glorious abundance" alluded to in Isaiah 66:11. We are drawn into God's bosom by a Savior who stretches out His own arms to welcome us home.

### She Would Learn alongside Him

The Shulammite isn't leading her Lover aimlessly, nor is she exerting inappropriate and demanding authority over him.

Read Song of Songs 8:2 again. Where is she leading him? Why?

She brings him, in hospitality, into her mother's home for a purpose. What's the purpose? Teaching and learning. Commentators are divided on whether the mother or Solomon is doing the teaching. Either way, this verse gives us a glimpse of what we need to know of the Shulammite's heart for our own study: *she herself is teachable*. The question we can ask ourselves is this: Are we teachable? Are we willing to let someone share an insight with us? Are we able to see where we have gone wrong and let grace change our hearts?

In what areas are you teachable? In what areas do you have a hard time acknowledging you could stand to grow and learn?

John 14:26 tells us where a teachable heart starts. Reference that verse to fill in the missing words below.

"The Father sends the _____ _____ to teach

us, in _____ name. He will _____ us all things and bring

to remembrance all that He has _____ _____

_____."

**2 TIMOTHY 3:16–17**
"All Scripture is breathed out by God and profitable for teaching, for reproof, for correction, and for training in righteousness, that the man of God may be complete, equipped for every good work."

The Holy Spirit teaches us through His voice in our lives, in and around the living and active Word of God, the Bible. We read, we listen, and we share His Word together, and true learning can begin only when we are in His Word.

### She Would Give Food and Drink to Him

## "I would give you spiced wine to drink, the juice of my pomegranate." Song of Songs 8:2b

I have no problem connecting with the Shulammite on this topic. I want my home to be a place where everyone feels welcome, whether it's over something as cheap and easy as a tall glass of iced coffee on a hot summer day or as festive and joyful as a holiday feast with tablecloths, special napkins, and the clink of wine glasses. But hospitality and entertaining, while good, can be intimidating for some, whether as the hostess or the guest.

In what ways can you share hospitality and relationship with others? If you do not enjoy hosting, in what ways can you share what you have been given in Christ without inviting people into your home?

What is your favorite way to invite people into your life, whether in your home or outside of it?

There are so many forms of hospitality and various ways in which to share who Jesus is with those around us! The Shulammite desires to give food and drink to her husband because she wants to fill him up with care and affection and invite him deeper into their relationship together.

What two items does she want to give her husband to drink?

Wine is never necessary. It's a luxury. We don't need it like we need water or vitamins found in juice, but it is a bounteous and aromatic gift from our Father in heaven. Yet, Jesus sat around a table with His disciples, hours before His crucifixion, and gave wine a greater purpose still—bestowing forgiveness.

God's great love is remarkable. He is the one who brings us in. He teaches us, He kisses us with the holy kiss of friendship, He nurses us and provides for us. He lavishes us with unimaginable love, and we respond to our Savior as the Shulammite responded to her Beloved.

Commentator Christopher Mitchell explains it like this: "Wine surpasses what is merely necessary to sustain life. It is a luxurious sign of God's blessing, and indication that the fallen creation can be and is being rejuvenated by his grace. It is a harbinger of better things in the age to come."[46]

# "OH, HOW I WANT TO BRING YOU INTO MY HOUSE, TO LOVE YOU IN RETURN, PRECIOUS SAVIOR!"

His love is always altogether beautiful.

## Inscribed upon My Heart

Use the Scripture memory verse for the week and the prayer prompt to bring your confession, thanksgiving, praise, and requests before the God who calls you beautiful.

### WEEK 7 MEMORY VERSE

"I am my beloved's, and his desire is for me. . . . Set me as a seal upon your heart, as a seal upon your arm, for love is strong as death, jealousy is fierce as the grave. Its flashes are flashes of fire, the very flame of the Lord." Song of Songs 7:10; 8:6

### PRAYER PROMPT

Dear Jesus, we are blessed with so many gifts from You, including . . .

# Day 3

We spent a good deal of time in our video lesson this last week discussing God's intense devotion for His people, His ardor as well as His jealousy. His devotion goes beyond our human understanding of relationship, and He loves us more than we can imagine. He is perfect justice. He is perfect love. And He is both equally, simultaneously. He does not shift with the winds and change His thoughts and emotions on a whim, like we do.

Read Song of Songs 8:6–7. What adjectives are used to describe love and jealousy?

## THE LORD, YAHWEH, THE GREAT I AM, IS BOTH PERFECT LOVE AND PERFECT JUSTICE.

What would the world look like without justice?

**1 JOHN 4:8B**
"God is love."

**ISAIAH 61:8A**
"For I, the LORD, love justice."

What would the world look like without love?

Because God is both love and justice, the very flame of the Lord flashes in both. We often want to see God as only love—a God who always accepts whatever we bring, who is always grace, always mercy. A loving God is more comfortable than a God who has rules and expectations. While we can come to God and stand before Him through Christ, we cannot experience His grace and mercy *without Christ*. We are sinners. We cannot bring our offering of sin nonchalantly before our good and perfect Father on our own.

Love is beautiful, and mercy is beautiful, but divine justice is also beautiful. God's justice coupled with God's love is God's Law and Gospel working together in blessed harmony. Think a few moments about the times in the Bible when we have seen God's justice—Adam and Eve's banishment from the garden, the great flood in Noah's time, even the loss of David and Bathsheba's firstborn son, Solomon's older brother.

What beauty and love is shown in God's justice in any of these examples?

Love and justice—God offers them both perfectly, in a way that may be hard for us to understand, because we ourselves can only act in love or justice imperfectly. In our lesson today, let's see how the two work together as the consuming fire of the Lord—that very flame of Yahweh.

Please look up the following verses and jot down how fire is connected to God in each passage. Think particularly about what aspects of justice and love God is showing in each passage.

| GOD IS JUSTICE | GOD IS LOVE |
|---|---|
| Deuteronomy 4:23–24 | |
| He is a consuming fire, a jealous God; when we build idols, He will destroy them. | He protects us from idolatry's destruction in our lives by setting some boundaries for us. |
| Nehemiah 9:17–19 | |
| | |
| Luke 9:53–55 | |
| | |
| Acts 2:2–4 | |
| | |
| Hebrews 12:26–29 | |
| | |

Good work! Looking through passages to discern and expand your understanding of who God is and what He does for us is no easy task. Can you see how often God used the image of fire and fire itself as tools to show who He is to His people? And these passages are just a few examples. From the Israelites wandering the desert with God's column of fire ever watching over them to our Lovers in the Song of Songs to the Holy Spirit poured out in lapping flames over the apostles' heads on Pentecost, all of these moments in time and history are meant to point to Christ Jesus.

In the Old Testament, God taught Israel to offer sacrifices as atonement for their sins. This pointed them to the bigger plan: Jesus Christ. Jesus is the true and complete sacrifice, put in the fire on the altar once and for all to atone for our sin. Hebrews 12:26–29, which you read a moment ago, assures us that the fire of the sacrifice itself is God's unfailing love, which cannot be shaken, cannot be snuffed out, but also cannot be ignored without consequence. Here stands the Law.

Fill in the missing words of Hebrews 12:26 below.

"At that time His voice shook the earth, but now He has promised,

'_____ _____

_____ I will shake not only the earth but also the

heavens.'"

God shook heaven and earth to rescue you. The Son of God came down to die for us, to sacrifice Himself in the flame of God's ardor, God's jealousy. Christ gave Himself. By His death on the cross, He fulfilled the devotion that God demanded from us. The whole earth shook, literally shook (Matthew 27:51), so that nothing could shake us from God's hand. In our lives, trouble may come and we may feel shaken, but we are secure in the gift of forgiveness and eternity because of Christ's sacrifice on the cross. The consuming fire of His love then came down to us on Pentecost, the love of God poured out on the people in Acts 2.

Read Acts 2:1–4. What was coupled with the fire?

> **"AT THAT TIME . . ."**
> There was a day on Mount Sinai when the law was given and the earth literally shook (Exodus 19:19). The law came, justice came, to open the door for grace.
>
> **"YET ONCE MORE . . ."**
> What a difference three little words make. Jesus changes everything. The earth shook at His death and His resurrection (Matthew 27:51; 28:2), so that we would be built on something unshakable, Christ's sacrifice, Christ's love, doing what we cannot do to save us from our sins.

That same fire is now found in us. God sent the Holy Spirit to fill us, guide us, give us solid ground, and give us feet that will not slip when the waves and challenges of life crash over us, when we feel shaken to the core. This, my friends, *this* is the Gospel.

How would you explain this complicated concept of God's love and justice to a friend? What hope is there in a God who has perfect love and perfect justice?

Perfect law and perfect grace . . . God's justice and His love is altogether beautiful.

## Inscribed upon My Heart

Use the Scripture memory verse for the week and the prayer prompt to bring your confession, thanksgiving, praise, and requests before the God who calls you beautiful.

### WEEK 7 MEMORY VERSE

"I am my beloved's, and his desire is for me. . . . Set me as a seal upon your heart, as a seal upon your arm, for love is strong as death, jealousy is fierce as the grave. Its flashes are flashes of fire, the very flame of the Lord." Song of Songs 7:10; 8:6

### PRAYER PROMPT

Christ Jesus, You are perfect love and perfect justice . . .

# Day 4

## PROTECTION AND PURPOSE IN LIFE TOGETHER
### SONG OF SONGS 8:8–9

Do you have a sister? If so, did you have a good relationship with your sister growing up? How is your relationship with your sister as an adult?

If you don't have a sister, did you long for one growing up? What makes a sister different from a brother?

I grew up with three sisters, all older than me. We played school, played a lot of soccer, and did a fair amount of mushroom hunting around the woods with our dad. But to my chagrin, there were two things my sisters did not enjoy playing—house and Barbies. I loved girly things. I had the giant Barbie mansion with several bedrooms but no one to create pretend drama with. At one point in our childhood, my sister who is closest in age to me actually made me sign a contract saying that if she played Barbies with me one more time, she would never have to play again . . . and she held me to it!

Even so, I thought my sisters were the coolest people who ever walked the planet. Coming from a blended family, I have one sister who was married before I was born, and two sisters came into my life when I was four years old. Sharing or not sharing the same blood never made them any more or less my sisters. God gave them to me as a gift, and from day one I wanted to be just like each of them. I wanted to style my hair like them and listen to the same music as them. I desperately wanted to be accepted and loved by them. I'm not sure they felt quite the same desperation I did for this reason: They were my big sisters. I was the little sister.

The Song of Songs teaches us something about little sisters. Let's read Song of Songs 8:8–9 to understand more. What descriptors can you find for this little sister?

Yes, it's the Others' turn again, but this time they speak in the very specific context of sisters. Commentators have differing views on who the Others are in this passage. Some commentators subscribe to the idea that the passage is the voice of the older brothers of the Shulammite from Song of Songs 1. Other commentators believe that while the Others are the same Daughters of Jerusalem we find in other passages, the "little sister" the Others speak of is a little sister of the Shulammite. Another possibility is that the Others are the same Daughters of Jerusalem gathered around one another, around a member of the Shulammite's extended family, or around Solomon's household. With all of this debating, the passage can get confusing quickly. So, we will focus on the meaty message of the passage rather than the who.

It is clear that the Others who speak are concerned for their *sister*, whether that sister is a blood relative, a cousin, a friend, or a metaphor for young women everywhere. The speakers address and proclaim their influence over her as she comes of age. This most certainly has implications for us as New Testament believers today.

Titus 2:1–8 gives us a clear picture of some things "big sisters and brothers" are to teach and share with their "little sisters and brothers." Besides age, how else might we understand "big" and "little" for teaching and sharing the faith?

List the characteristics given in Titus 2:1–8 of the older men and women that are fruits of faith from the Holy Spirit.

How has someone shared or taught any of these things to you?

How can you share these things organically or teach them intentionally to those little brothers or sisters around you, those newer to the faith?

How open are you at this time to being taught by those around you who are more mature in faith? Circle the number that best describes where you think you are in your willingness to be taught. There is no judgment here. This question just helps you be honest with yourself. Your answer does not need to be shared with anyone if you do not feel comfortable doing so.

| I am completely closed to being taught by others in the faith. | 0 1 2 3 4 5 6 7 8 9 10 | I love to be taught by others in the faith and regularly seek it out. |
| --- | --- | --- |

Sometimes I find myself at an 8 or a 9—"Super open!" At other times, I know I am lacking and in need of forgiveness for thinking more highly of myself than I ought. Whether I ignore the wisdom of my fellow brothers and sisters in Christ or avoid Bible study because of busyness, I usually pay for it later as my life feels more harried and my attitude becomes such that I should check it at the door. Yet Christ's forgiveness is always ready for us when we repent of the times we have tried to go it on our own. We can also pray for God to keep our ears attuned to wisdom from mature brothers and sisters around us.

In Song of Songs 8, the bigs sisters are concerned for the little sister's purity, in particular, her chastity. We, too, need others to help us remain pure in our lives—to discern the purity of God's Word from Satan's lies, true from false, and "sort of sounds like what God would say" from "God says this." Keep in mind, however, that not every believer is a "big" brother or sister. Titus warns us that there is a lot of unsound theology and direction out there—and plenty of confusion (1:10).

**CHASTITY**
The art of refraining. How can we help women younger or less mature than we are to refrain from things that would harm them in the long run?

To whom do you go when you need help figuring out the truth of God in your life? What makes this person a trustworthy source?

Mary, as a young pregnant mother bearing the Son of God in her womb, had Elizabeth to encourage her, to be a big sister to her.

Read Luke 1:39–56. What encouragement or wisdom might Mary have gleaned from her visit with Elizabeth?

What a joy to be women in the Church today! We have the blessing of one another. When my children are squirming in the pew and refuse to stay in Bible study childcare, I have women who pass those not-so-cutie-pies around until the children are bubbling over with joy. When I am angry with my husband, whether for real reasons or reasons I made up in my head, I have women in my life who help me to put the best perspective on the situation and speak tenderly and kindly to me—and also of him. When I feel beaten down by the world, saddened and hard-hearted over sin and all the evil in the world, I have women who raise up the cross of Christ Jesus before me and invite me into prayer.

Let's not trade in these relationships for fear and frustration over past bad advice and broken relationships. Rather, let's form and nurture these relationships around the Word of God, the best source for discernment. He who begins a good work in you begins a good work in your relationships as well.

Which young woman or women need you to hem them in with Jesus' love and care? On which topics in particular do you think young women need guidance?

His work in us and through us, in the family of faith and the world around us, is altogether beautiful.

# Inscribed upon My Heart

Use the Scripture memory verse for the week and the prayer prompt to bring your confession, thanksgiving, praise, and requests before the God who calls you beautiful.

## WEEK 7 MEMORY VERSE

"I am my beloved's, and his desire is for me. . . . Set me as a seal upon your heart, as a seal upon your arm, for love is strong as death, jealousy is fierce as the grave. Its flashes are flashes of fire, the very flame of the Lord." Song of Songs 7:10; 8:6

## PRAYER PROMPT

Lord, be with all the women in my life. Help me to care for and build up . . .

# Day 5

## ONEFLESHNESS AND OTHER MADE-UP WORDS
### SONG OF SONGS 8:8–12

We have come to our last day of daily study in the Song of Songs. Well done! Flip back through the pages of your workbook and see all that you have completed. See your answers to the questions, your own writing filling the space on the pages.

What is the concept that has taken firm root in your heart and mind during this study? What one thing rises above the rest?

**ISAIAH 55:11**
"So shall My word be that goes out from My mouth; it shall not return to Me empty, but it shall accomplish that which I purpose, and shall succeed in the thing for which I sent it."

Hallelujah! He is surely at work. What does Isaiah 55:11 promise us?

God's Word goes out into our lives, into our relationships, into our homes, into our workplaces, into our churches—and He accomplishes His purposes. It's a beautiful thing.

Look back at Song of Songs 4:7. Write the theme verse for our entire study in the space below.

This work, the things that Christ is doing in your life today, they are altogether beautiful to Him. You are altogether beautiful to Him. Not just a little bit beautiful, but *altogether* beautiful.

Today's reading from the Song of Songs feels like one of the oddest to me, so if you are thrown off, you are not alone. In fact, it's so odd that I made up a word to describe what is going on here: *onefleshness*. Song of Songs 8:8–12 teaches us not just about the concept of one flesh in marriage but also the art of living in onefleshness.

Please read Song of Songs 8:8–12. (We'll study verses 13 and 14 in our last video together.) Write out anything related to numbers in the passage.

Why all the tallying of money and the vineyard?

Consider the broader story of the Song of Songs. In Song of Songs 1:6, we met a young woman whose brothers forced her to tend the family vineyard. In these concluding verses, we see a woman who is one with her husband and who has thousands of acres of vineyards and keepers aplenty. All the talk of many vineyards and much fruit, however, points to a greater reality of the Shulammite's life—and our lives.

She was only intended for one. We were only intended for one.

Let's consider context. Song of Songs 8:8–9 is unmistakably about purity—the little sister, the door, the wall. In verse 10, we see the Shulammite's response. We also see doors and walls a little differently because she acknowledges her own transition from an unmarried chaste woman to a woman who enjoys all the fruits of married life, a onefleshness with her husband. Within this context, the message of the next couple of verses is not "don't" but the Gospel of "do" in marriage. The Shulammite tells us that she gives *all* of herself to her husband, fully, wholeheartedly, with abandon.

Fill in the missing words of Song of Songs 8:12 below to see this truth more clearly.

"My vineyard, _____  _____  _____,

is before me; you, O Solomon, _____  _____

the thousand, and the keepers of the fruit two hundred. "

She is "one who finds peace," we read in verse 10, which is an indication of her married status. She has found the one whom her soul loves (Song of Songs 3:4). Now, she proclaims that what she has, her very own vineyard, is Solomon's.

## "You, O Solomon, may have . . . " Song of Songs 8:12

The Shulammite's experience shares biblical truth. It helps us to remember that two become one in every sense of the word in marriage—it's more than just a nice idea about sex. And whether we are the girl from chapter 1, longing to share our vineyard of life, or the fully satisfied matron of peace we find in chapter 8, we have something to learn. Let's hash it out.

What is the difference between a door and a wall?

In week 3, we learned about Jerusalem's walls, designed for undergoing months of siege by intruding nations. Doors, even in the wall itself, let people in. The doors gave access to the city from the outside, both for the economy's sake (shepherds and farmers who worked in the fields) and for relationship's sake (visiting family from far away who needed to get in). Likewise, we have the opportunity to open doors in our lives. We make friendships. We offer trust inside and outside of our families. We create a door for people to know us, the real us. This is a gift of God—doors to one another's lives.

We are also given the gift of walls in our relationships. We construct walls, in a way, when we construct boundaries. When relationships are harmful to us, when people misuse us or they have an influence over our lives that does not reflect Christ, walls are necessary. This is vitally important in any relationship, but consider the necessity of walls particularly in our very intimate and sexual relationships. The language of the Shulammite's brothers and/or sisters in Song of Songs 8:8, and then her own in Song of Songs 8:9, reflects the importance of not just a boundary line but thick walls in regard to our body outside of the one-flesh marriage relationship.

I could go on for hours about the physical, chemical, emotional, and spiritual consequences of sex with someone other than our spouse,[47] but at some point we have to decide between believing God and believing man. The Song of Songs gives us the opportunity to come face-to-face with what we believe God says about relationships. The walls-and-doors concept of our passage is a great reminder of what we know from the rest of Scripture. While God offers boundless love and forgiveness for all our sins, He is also very clear on the consequences of sex before or outside of marriage: it will hurt us. It destroys, it shatters, it breaks. This could not be more countercultural. Walls should be the language of the unmarried as well as the married. Trying to resurrect a city wall after the battering ram of casual sex has beaten it down is big work, hard labor—not fixed with a simple brushstroke of "no big deal" that the world tries to sell as a fix-it. God's rescue from our sin is a promise that is sure and certain. Praise the Lord! He heals, but let's not pretend that sin isn't painful.

So, where's the Gospel? What wisdom would you share with a friend struggling with something?

What is the grace of giving all of yourself to your spouse alone?

Physical connection and intimacy are such a beautiful gift from our God. They build up the one-flesh relationship in a unique and desirable way. *Lord, thank You for Your gifts, as well as Your forgiveness. Thank You, Savior, for knowing exactly what we need and when. We lift up our hearts and our lives to You alone.*

As we move on through the Song to verses 11 and 12, we find a broader view of what "one flesh" means. We could talk about physical intimacy until the cows come home, and we would still only be touching on a small slice of the mystery of one flesh. Read Song of Songs 8:11–12 again. The Shulammite's message to Solomon is this: *you can have it all, darling.*

Let's explore some realms of onefleshness.

In what ways do you think couples become one flesh? Consider the different parts of the whole person (vocations, emotions, spiritual growth, intellect, etc.).

There may not be a specific right answer. God invites us to work this out for ourselves with Him, studying His Word for truth to apply to our lives.

# "This mystery is profound." Ephesians 5:32

When God declares that something is a mystery for us, He also invites us to discovery in His Word. That's one of the most awesome joys of the one-flesh relationship when you're in it—discovery. We wouldn't want to miss this as a joy of life outside of marriage too, particularly in our relationship with God. We get to see God and discover more about Him in many unique ways: through Christ, His Son; through His Word; through His Bride, the Church; and through marriages around you that demonstrate Christ's love for His people. Throughout these last seven weeks, Solomon and his bride have given us one picture of onefleshness. The Song of Songs teaches us the value of being a part of all the relationships around us and learning and growing together.

Marriage may or may not be in God's plans for you, but I would hate for you to miss the full picture of Christ and the Church by not observing marriages around you.

What can you learn from the marriages around you, whether you are married or not?

Whose marriage story speaks the life-giving work of Christ into your life?

Solomon and an unknown Shulammite—this couple in a tiny and seemingly irrelevant book of the Old Testament—teach us that our God gives *all of Himself* to us. In His Spirit, we can begin to give all of ourselves to Him. One day, Christ and His Church will join together completely as one flesh, in that perfect unity that is only a mystery to us now. When Christ returns, we will behold His face. He will hold us close. We'll talk more about Christ coming back for the Bride in our final video, but until then, let's close our study by writing out the words of our memory verse for the week.

Please write Song of Songs 8:6 below.

His love is so fierce for you—no matter your marital status, no matter your life stage or place, no matter the season of glory or season of struggle you're in. His fierce love, His testimony written across marriages and lives everywhere—from Solomon and the Shulammite to Marv and Marcella to your own marriage or the marriage of someone close to you—is altogether beautiful, friends, *altogether beautiful.*

## INSCRIBED UPON MY HEART

Rewrite this week's Scripture memory verse below one last time, and while you do, praise His holy name for being in the midst of the waiting.

### WEEK 7 MEMORY VERSE

"I am my beloved's, and his desire is for me. . . . Set me as a seal upon your heart, as a seal upon your arm, for love is strong as death, jealousy is fierce as the grave. Its flashes are flashes of fire, the very flame of the LORD." Song of Songs 7:10; 8:6

### PRAYER PROMPT

Lord, please bring Your life-giving beauty where I cannot see it, especially . . .

# Your Identity in Christ

## 30-Day Reading Plan

To encourage you to remain in God's Word daily, here's a reading plan that will remind you of who you are in Christ. Whether you choose to start this reading plan now or tear it out and save it for another time, I encourage you open your Bibles and write the titles given to you by God near the Scripture passages listed. May you always remember who you are in Christ!

| | | |
|---|---|---|
| **DAY 1** | **DAY 11** | **DAY 21** |
| New<br>2 Corinthians 5:17 | Child<br>1 John 3:1 | Full of hope<br>Romans 15:4 |
| **DAY 2** | **DAY 12** | **DAY 22** |
| Redeemed<br>1 Peter 1:18–19 | Friend<br>John 15:15 | Healed<br>Psalm 147:3 |
| **DAY 3** | **DAY 13** | **DAY 23** |
| His<br>Isaiah 43:1 | Written on His palm<br>Isaiah 49:16 | Loved<br>Jeremiah 31:3 |
| **DAY 4** | **DAY 14** | **DAY 24** |
| Righteous<br>1 Corinthians 1:30 | Chosen<br>1 Thessalonians 1:4 | Alive<br>Ephesians 2:4–5 |
| **DAY 5** | **DAY 15** | **DAY 25** |
| Created<br>Genesis 1:27 | Holy<br>Colossians 1:2 | Not forgotten<br>Isaiah 49:15 |
| **DAY 6** | **DAY 16** | **DAY 26** |
| Rescued<br>Colossians 1:13 | Wonderful<br>Psalm 139:14 | Called for a purpose<br>Romans 8:28 |
| **DAY 7** | **DAY 17** | **DAY 27** |
| An integral part<br>1 Corinthians 12:17 | Worth dying for<br>Galatians 2:20 | Strong<br>Isaiah 40:31 |
| **DAY 8** | **DAY 18** | **DAY 28** |
| Royal<br>1 Peter 2:9 | Citizen of heaven<br>Philippians 3:20 | Comforted<br>2 Corinthians 1:5 |
| **DAY 9** | **DAY 19** | **DAY 29** |
| Free<br>Galatians 5:1 | No longer condemned<br>Romans 8:1 | Heard<br>Psalm 94:9 |
| **DAY 10** | **DAY 20** | **DAY 30** |
| For His glory<br>Ephesians 1:12 | Forgiven<br>Ephesians 1:7 | Beautiful<br>Song of Songs 4:7 |

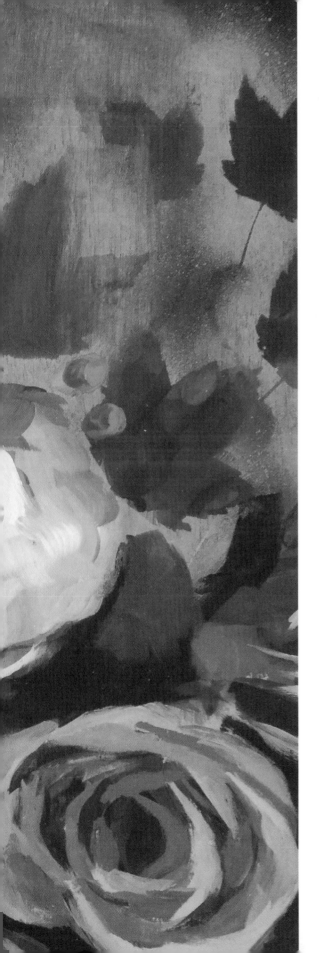

# WEEK 8

MAKE HASTE!

# Viewer Guide

VIDEO 8: MAKE HASTE
**SONG OF SONGS 8:13–14**

**VERSES TO BOOKMARK**
Song of Songs 8:13–14
Hebrews 10:19–23
Revelation 22:16–20

The ending of the Song of Songs is really no ending at all. It's really all about new beginnings.

Song of Songs 8:13–14:

"O you who dwell in the gardens,

    with companions listening for your voice;

    let me hear it.

Make haste, my beloved,

    and be like a gazelle

or a young stag

    on the mountains of spices."

**HASTEN**
To hurry, to run, to leap, to be quick about it, to move urgently.

One phrase points to a bigger, grander picture than we could even imagine: "make haste."

The story doesn't _____ here for us or for Solomon and his bride.

## THREE WAYS GOD HASTENS

1. GOD HASTENS _____ _____.

Christ came once to make you _____, but He also comes to make you _____.

    "Even if it was just you, if you were the only one, He would have died for you."

2. GOD HASTENS TO CREATE _____ _____ _____.

Hebrews 10:19: "_____, brothers, _____ we have confidence to enter the holy places by the blood of _____ . . ."

3. GOD HASTENS TO CREATE _____ _____ _____.

God created the Church for our benefit. He gives us the gift of one another.

## IN THE MEANTIME . . .

We wait _____ _____.

The plea of "Make haste!" insinuates a real desire for Him to hurry it up!

Remember, Christ makes us _____, but He also makes us _____.

## "You are altogether beautiful, my love; there is no flaw in you." Song of Songs 4:7

In Christ, we are _____, altogether beautiful, but this side of heaven we are also _____.

The Song of Songs seems so _____ because *our* story is not _____.

**AUTHOR'S NOTE**
Some things in life leave us asking Jesus to wait a little longer to come—watching our children grow, wanting to get married, or other professional or personal goals. Life is good, and God gives it so much meaning! But when Jesus comes back, it will be beyond our wildest imagination, with no tears, no sin, no loss. This is why we rest in these words: "Make haste. Come quickly, Lord Jesus."

Each day, let us seek Christ and ask Him to bring the completion of the whole story for which we wait.

In the meantime, we pray together, "*Make haste, beloved. Amen. Come, Lord Jesus. . . . You are altogether beautiful, Savior. Altogether beautiful, Lord.*"

**REVELATION 22:12**
"Behold, I am coming soon."

## DISCUSSION QUESTIONS

1. What things in the world make you intensely aware that you would like Jesus to hasten in coming for us?

2. How do our family relationships shape how we view God? What Bible passages come to mind that support the truth of who God is? How do these passages connect accurately or inaccurately with what you learned in your family?

3. What is altogether beautiful in this life? What altogether beautiful things do you anticipate in the next?

# In the Meantime . . .

Waiting is hard.

Sometimes in life we are called to wait for more than a doctor's appointment. We wait for the future, we wait for the next season, we wait for struggles to pass. In Song of Songs 8:13-14, God asks us to wait for something bigger—for His physical return to us, when all pain will be gone and we'll see Him face-to-face.

So, what are some of the promises of God in the waiting? What can we lean on when we look around at a world that hurts so much and does not know the redemption of a Savior who loves us so? There are many. I want to share three of them with you that I lean on almost daily.

## WE HAVE AN ANCHOR.

"We have this as a sure and steadfast anchor of the soul, a hope that enters into the inner place behind the curtain, where Jesus has gone as a forerunner on our behalf, having become a high priest forever after the order of Melchizedek." (Hebrews 6:19–20)

Bring it on, storms of life. We have an anchor to hold us steady, even when it feels like things are falling apart. We know this life isn't all there is, and Christ Jesus holds us.

## HIS LOVE NEVER, NEVER FAILS.

"Who shall separate us from the love of Christ? Shall tribulation, or distress, or persecution, or famine, or nakedness, or danger, or sword? As it is written, 'For Your sake we are being killed all the day long; we are regarded as sheep to be slaughtered.' No, in all these things we are more than conquerors through Him who loved us. For I am sure that neither death nor life, nor angels nor rulers, nor things present nor things to come, nor powers, nor height nor depth, nor anything else in all creation, will be able to separate us from the love of God in Christ Jesus our Lord." (Romans 8:35–39)

Nothing. Nothing can separate us from God's love—nothing in us, nothing in the world, and nothing that walks into our lives uninvited. Did I say nothing? Nothing can come between His love for you and your spirit!

## HE HEARS OUR PRAYERS.

"And this is the confidence that we have toward Him, that if we ask anything according to His will He hears us." (1 John 5:14)

He does hear us! The Lovers of the Song of Songs teach us that intimacy in relationships is important. There are times in the Song when everything else melts away for each of them. It's just them, together. Not everything in which we see God has to be miraculous. He works in the simple. He works in the mundane. He works in the day-to-day. He works in our various vocations and communities and families. He is writing the story of each of our lives with His own hand, while we wait.

# About the Author

Deaconess Heidi Goehmann is the founder of I Love My Shepherd and ilovemyshepherd.com, which strive to provide resources that are intensely theological while remaining intensely practical, and help women get into the Word daily. I Love My Shepherd also advocates for women, marriages, and individuality through its articles and podcast.

Heidi is a licensed independent social worker and mental health care provider, a writer, speaker, wife, mom, and forgiven and loved child of God. She received her deaconess certification, as well as her bachelor's degree, from Concordia University Chicago, and her master's degree in social work is from the University of Toledo with an emphasis on children, families, and social justice.

Heidi has worked in a variety of clinical settings, including trauma treatment for abuse and sexual assault, cross-cultural research, Eye Movement Desensitization and Reprocessing, and home-based therapy. She has also served in various ministry capacities, including college student ministry, women's and children's ministry, and mission work.

Heidi's passions include her husband, David; her kids, Macee, Jonah, Jyeva, and Ezekiel; and red wine, dark chocolate, Jesus, Star Trek, Star Wars, and new ideas . . . not necessarily in that order.

# A Note of Thanks

No study or book ever comes together on its own through the work of one person. This is never truer than in His Body—you and I, we can't do this work alone, or this life alone, for that matter.

Thank you to my family, who sends me out, even when it means reheated soup for days.

Thank you to my mom, my dad, and my sisters for loving me through life when I didn't think I was worthy, beautiful, or savable.

Thank you to my "Others" who cheer me on, comfort my tears when I am frustrated, and listen without judging. You know who you are.

Thank you to Elizabeth, Barbara, Laura, and the entire CPH team for seeing a writer in me when I did not see one in myself.

And thank you to a small group of pastors' wives who suffered through the infancy of this study so that it could turn into what it is today.

You are each altogether beautiful to me.

# Endnotes

1   Pelikan, Jaroslav, ed. "Lectures on the Song of Solomon," *Luther's Works*, American Edition, vol. 15 (St. Louis: Concordia Publishing House, 1972), 191–264.

2   Mitchell, Christopher W. *The Song of Songs*, Concordia Commentary, Dean O. Wenthe ed. (St. Louis: Concordia Publishing House, 2003), 547.

3   Ehlke, Roland C. *Song of Songs*, People's Bible Commentary (St. Louis: Concordia Publishing House, 1992, 2004), 135.

4   From the Holy Bible, New Living Translation, copyright © 1996, 2004, 2007, 2013, 2015 by Tyndale House Foundation. Used by permission of Tyndale House Publishers, Inc., Carol Stream, Illinois 60188. All rights reserved.

5   Henry, Matthew. "Song of Solomon." *Matthew Henry's Concise Commentary*. www.biblegateway.com/resources/matthew-henry/Song-of-Solomon, accessed June 12, 2017.

6   Ehlke, Roland C. *Song of Songs*, People's Bible Commentary (St. Louis: Concordia Publishing House, 1992, 2004), 135.

7   Lewis, C. S. The Four Loves. (New York: Harper Collins One, 1960), 155. THE FOUR LOVES by C. S. Lewis copyright © C. S. Lewis Pte. Ltd. 1960. Extract reprinted by permission.

8   Engelbrecht, Edward A., general ed., *The Lutheran Study Bible* [ESV] (St. Louis: Concordia Publishing House, 2009), 1067.

9   Engelbrecht, Edward A., general ed., *The Lutheran Study Bible* [ESV] (St. Louis: Concordia Publishing House, 2009), 1066.

10  Mitchell, Christopher W. *The Song of Songs*, Concordia Commentary, Dean O. Wenthe ed. (St. Louis: Concordia Publishing House, 2003), 610–12.

11  Ehlke, Roland C. *Song of Songs*, People's Bible Commentary (St. Louis: Concordia Publishing House, 1992, 2004), 148.

12  "Bible Hub Interlinear Bible." http://biblehub.com/interlinear/, accessed June 13, 2017.

13  Engelbrecht, Edward A., general ed., *The Lutheran Study Bible* [ESV] (St. Louis: Concordia Publishing House, 2009), 1067.

14  Engelbrecht, Edward A., general ed., *The Lutheran Study Bible* [ESV] (St. Louis: Concordia Publishing House, 2009), 1066.

15  Mitchell, Christopher W. *The Song of Songs*, Concordia Commentary, Dean O. Wenthe ed. (St. Louis: Concordia Publishing House, 2003), 669.

16  "Bible Hub Interlinear Bible." http://biblehub.com/hebrew/1714.htm, accessed June 13, 2017.

17  Engelbrecht, Edward A., general ed., *The Lutheran Study Bible* [ESV] (St. Louis: Concordia Publishing House, 2009), 1069.

18  Pelikan, Jaroslav, ed., "Lectures on the Song of Solomon," *Luther's Works*, American Edition, vol. 15 (St. Louis: Concordia Publishing House, 1972), 216.

19  "Biblehub Interlinear Bible." http://biblehub.com/hebrew/7650.htm, accessed September 24, 2017.

20  Ehlke, Roland C. *Song of Songs*, People's Bible Commentary (St. Louis: Concordia Publishing House, 1992, 2004), 159–60.

21  Mitchell, Christopher W. *The Song of Songs*, Concordia Commentary, Dean O. Wenthe ed. (St. Louis: Concordia Publishing House, 2003), 698.

22  Gottman, John M. and Nan Silver. *Seven Principles for Making Marriage Work* (New York: Harmony Books, 1999), 26–27.

23  "Bible Hub Interlinear Bible." http://biblehub.com/hebrew/6965.htm, accessed June 13, 2017.

24  "Bible Hub Interlinear Bible." http://biblehub.com/hebrew/3615.htm, accessed June 13, 2017.

25  Lewis, C. S. *The Weight of Glory* (New York: Harper Collins One, 1980), 26. THE WEIGHT OF GLORY by C. S. Lewis copyright © C. S. Lewis Pte. Ltd. 1949. Extract reprinted by permission.

26  Frances R. Havergal, 1836–79, public domain.

27  Copyright © 2011 Thank you Music (PRS) (adm. worldwide at CapitolCMGPublishing.com excluding Europe which is adm. by

Integrity Music, part of the David C Cook family. Songs@integritymusic.com) / worshiptogether.com Songs (ASCAP) sixsteps Music (ASCAP) Sweater Weather Music (ASCAP) Valley Of Songs Music (BMI) (adm. at CapitolCMGPublishing .com). All rights reserved. Used by permission.

28  Henry, Matthew. "Song of Solomon," *Matthew Henry's Concise Commentary*. https://www.biblegateway.com/resources/ matthew-henry/Song-of-Solomon, accessed July 3, 2017.

29  Engelbrecht, Edward A., general ed. *The Lutheran Study Bible* [ESV] (St. Louis: Concordia Publishing House, 2009), xxxvi–xxxvii.

30  Pelikan, Jaroslav, ed. "Lectures on the Song of Solomon," Luther's Works, American Edition, vol. 15 (St. Louis: Concordia Publishing House, 1972), 231.

31  Henry, Matthew. "Song of Solomon," *Matthew Henry's Concise Commentary*. www .biblegateway.com/resources/matthew-henry/Song-of-Solomon, accessed July 3, 2017.

32  Mitchell, Christopher W. *The Song of Songs*, Concordia Commentary, Dean O. Wenthe ed. (St. Louis: Concordia Publishing House, 2003), 829–32.

33  Engelbrecht, Edward A., general ed. *The Lutheran Study Bible* [ESV] (St. Louis: Concordia Publishing House, 2009), xxxvi–xxxvii.

34  "Bible Hub NASB Lexicon." http://biblehub. com/lexicon/songs/5-7.htm, accessed August 24, 2017.

35  Engelbrecht, Edward A., general ed. *The Lutheran Study Bible* [ESV] (St. Louis: Concordia Publishing House, 2009), 1123.

36  *Lutheran Service Book* (St. Louis: Concordia Publishing House, 2006), 618. Text © 1941 Concordia Publishing House. Used by permission.

37  "Names and Titles of God." *WebBible Encyclopedia*. http://www.christiananswers. net/dictionary/namesofgod.html accessed on July 15, 2017.

38  bibleresources.org/, accessed on July 15, 2017.

39  "Jesus Christ, titles and names of." *Dictionary of Bible Themes*. https://www .biblegateway.com/resources/dictionary-of-bible-themes/2203-Jesus-Christ-titles-names, accessed on July 15, 2017.

40  Engelbrecht, Edward A., general ed. *The Lutheran Study Bible* [ESV] (St. Louis: Concordia Publishing House, 2009), 2218.

41  Mitchell, Christopher W. *The Song of Songs*. Concordia Commentary Series, Dean O. Wenthe, ed. (St. Louis: Concordia Publishing House, 2003), 1016.

42  "Bible Hub Interlinear Bible." https:// biblehub.com/hebrew/5577.htm, accessed August 25, 2017.

43  "Bible Hub Interlinear Bible." http:// biblehub.com/hebrew/3045.htm, accessed on July 25, 2017.

44  Henry, Matthew. "Song of Solomon," *Matthew Henry's Concise Commentary*. https://www.biblegateway.com/resources/ matthew-henry/Song-of-Solomon, accessed June 12, 2017.

45  Mitchell, Christopher W. *The Song of Songs*, Concordia Commentary, Dean O. Wenthe ed. (St. Louis: Concordia Publishing House, 2003), 1153–62.

46  Mitchell, Christopher W. *The Song of Songs*, Concordia Commentary, Dean O. Wenthe ed. (St. Louis: Concordia Publishing House, 2003), 1167.

47  See Joe S. McIlhaney Jr. and Freda McKissich Bush, *Hooked: New Science on How Casual Sex Is Affecting Our Children* (Chicago: Northfield Publishing, 2008).